"This is a love story. Margot [...] you to imagine the limitless [...] you hear the whisper of God's love, and [...] become that whisper to the world."

> Shane Claiborne, activist, author, www.thesimpleway.org

"Margot Starbuck has done it again. With humor, honesty, and grace, she identifies a central problem within evangelical Christianity and she offers an invitation to the way of Jesus, the way of truth and grace."

> Amy Julia Becker, author of *A Good and Perfect Gift*

"I genuinely love *Permission Granted* by Margot Starbuck. I love it not just for its message of authentically reclaiming how Jesus would love and engage today's world, but more so because I know Margot lives out exactly what she writes. I can only hope that one day the Christian publishing world would be filled *only* with books from people like Margot. Please read *Permission Granted* and let it compel you, as it did me, to love in the tension that exists all around us."

> Andrew Marin, author of the award-winning book
> *Love Is an Orientation*, www.themarinfoundation.org

"Living out the Great Commandment requires embracing a counter-cultural lifestyle. With this book, Margot Starbuck offers specific directives and a host of wonderful stories to back up her message that Christlike loving is not only at the heart of this lifestyle but is the basis of meaningful living."

> Tony Campolo, PhD, Professor Emeritus,
> Eastern University

"In her book *Permission Granted* Margot Starbuck writes about the 'Rare Religious'—Christians who love sinners well. Since Jesus was called a 'friend of sinners' and we claim to follow him, loving sinners shouldn't be rare. Unfortunately, it is. And that's why this book is a necessary challenge that we Christ-followers need."

> Vince Antonucci, pastor of Verve Church,
> Las Vegas; author of *Renegade*

# permission granted

and other thoughts on
living graciously among
sinners and saints

## Margot Starbuck

**BakerBooks**

*a division of Baker Publishing Group*
Grand Rapids, Michigan

Published by Baker Books
a division of Baker Publishing Group
P.O. Box 6287, Grand Rapids, MI 49516-6287
www.bakerbooks.com

Printed in the United States of America

Library of Congress Cataloging-in-Publication Data is on file at the Library of Congress, Washington, DC.

ISBN 978-0-8010-1493-2

Unless otherwise indicated, Scripture quotations are from the Holy Bible, New International Version®. NIV®. Copyright © 1973, 1978, 1984, 2011 by Biblica, Inc.™ Used by permission of Zondervan. All rights reserved worldwide. www.zondervan.com

Scripture quotations labeled Message are from *The Message* by Eugene H. Peterson, copyright © 1993, 1994, 1995, 2000, 2001, 2002. Used by permission of NavPress Publishing Group. All rights reserved.

Scripture quotations labeled NLT are from the Holy Bible, New Living Translation, copyright © 1996, 2004, 2007 by Tyndale House Foundation. Used by permission of Tyndale House Publishers, Inc., Carol Stream, Illinois 60188. All rights reserved.

Scripture quotations labeled NRSV are from the New Revised Standard Version of the Bible, copyright © 1989, by the Division of Christian Education of the National Council of the Churches of Christ in the United States of America. Used by permission. All rights reserved.

To protect the privacy of those who have shared their stories with the author, some details and names have been changed.

The internet addresses, email addresses, and phone numbers in this book are accurate at the time of publication. They are provided as a resource. Baker Publishing Group does not endorse them or vouch for their content or permanence.

13  14  15  16  17  18  19     7  6  5  4  3  2  1

For Pam and for Geri

Thank you for your wildly
unconditional love for me,
exactly as I am.

God loves you unconditionally,
as you are and not as you should be,
because nobody is as they should be.

Brennan Manning

# contents

Introduction: The Unlikely Way   9

1. Naptime Revelations   13

2. Sloppy Dog Love   23

3. Internal Consistency and Secrets for Manipulating People   31

4. When the Church Plays Weird Theological Twister   41

5. Viscerally Repellant People Who Deserve the Sour Lemon Face   51

6. Little Bit Better Than the Other Guy   59

7. A Fun Party Trick   67

8. Friend-O'-Sinners Jesus Action Figure   77

9. Who Even Knew about Exclusive Paganists?   87

10. Three Fingers Pointing Back at Me   97

11. The Nutty Logic    103

12. Wordless Communication    113

13. Baby Killers and the Surprise of Identifying with
    Monstrous Sinners    121

14. Clarifying My Job Description    135

15. Jesus in Vegas    143

16. Report as Abuse    153

17. Live Women on Display and Other Disturbing
    Maladies    163

18. Living with Bossy (or Why We've Simply Got to Do
    More Judging)    173

19. Two-Headed Baby Born in Brazil    181

20. Moving toward People Who Really Matter    193

21. Double the Strategy    205

22. Fred Phelps Funeral    211

23. Condoning, Condemning, and Loving What Is    225

24. The Moment Ted Haggard Went Home Justified    233

25. Until the Fat Lady Sings    241

26. Truth. Love. Lies.    249

27. The One Who Is    257


Notes    267

# introduction

## the unlikely way

My friend Andy tells a story about a church situated along the route of the annual Gay Pride parade in Chicago whose members show up each year to protest the festivities. As the parade marches by, they wave an assortment of hand-lettered placards that include:

This awkward snapshot, to everyone else if not to us, is a high-def mug shot of how the Religious, until now, have engaged with folks we've identified as "Special Sinners." Sometimes, with the best of intentions, we've communicated that even though *we* don't accept their behavior, God loves and accepts these Sinners just as they are. Then we're baffled—sometimes *vehemently* baffled—when the Sinners don't believe us.

And yet I keep meeting folks who are itchy to live differently.

These Christians really *want* to embrace their neighbors who've been identified by the Religious as sinful. Convinced that Jesus wouldn't initiate relationships with a doctrinal placard, they desperately want to *love* differently.

They want to love like Jesus.

This, however, is not as easy as it might seem at first blush. Having been raised Religious, I can certainly identify with the sometimes awkward among us. In our linoleum-tiled Sunday school classrooms, we learned early to distinguish the Righteous from the Sinners. Contrary to the suspicions of our critics, there were no malevolent instructors teaching little children to condemn. Rather, that script of separation between righteous and unrighteous, sinner and saint, was actually woven throughout our holy book.

As preteens we were warned to keep a safe distance from the lures of the world: alcohol, drugs, and sex. Given our developmental fragility, it wasn't bad advice. Logically, then, we were most likely to succeed if we also separated ourselves from those who didn't keep such a safe distance from alcohol, drugs, and sex. This safe distance, however, made the actual practice of loving anyone whose behavior didn't mirror ours more than a little unwieldy.

As we moved into adulthood we understood clearly that loving God and loving people were our cardinal directives. Unfortunately, we simply had no idea how to engage with the people we'd always been warned to avoid.

Most of us recognize that the postures of "Christians" in some of the outrageous snapshots touted by the media—spewing vitriol at military funerals, threatening to burn Korans, demeaning gay people from Sunday morning pulpits—are alarmingly dissimilar from the ones we've been given of Jesus in the Gospels. It does not require any sophisticated theological training to recognize the discrepancies.

The Gospel examples of Jesus looked very different from anything I'd ever seen practiced by the Religious. Instead of backing away cautiously, the way I like to do, Jesus moved toward those who'd been identified as disreputable Sinners. Not only did he not treat them as being worth less than the Righteous, the way I'd been groomed to do, he actually went to a lot of trouble to insist that these Sinners were worth so much that his Father spared no expense in his dogged pursuit of them. His unexpected behavior both surprised his closest friends and outraged the Religious.

Sadly, the passing of centuries has made this distinctly Christian form of love no more prevalent and no less scandalous.

Frankly, this messy business of loving those who've been identified as Special Sinners—whatever that canon includes for you—requires a good measure of godly courage because it is more concerned for the heart of the other than it is with the image of the self. Scott Bessenecker, author of *The New Friars*, paints a picture in which Sinners are seen with both spiritual and physical eyes as beautiful and worthy of unconditional love.

"I once visited Rahab Ministry, an outreach to prostitutes in Bangkok," Bessenecker begins.

They have opened up a beauty shop in the Patpong district, one of the most notorious red-light districts in the city. The volunteers with Rahab do up the prostitutes before they go out. At first glance this seems counterproductive for an

11

organization determined to deliver prostitutes from a life of selling their bodies to strangers. However, in the process of making up prostitutes, Rahab workers (some of them former prostitutes themselves) have been able to build relationships of trust among the sex workers of Patpong. They have introduced many of their prostitute friends to Jesus and have called them to a better way of life, not from a position of superiority, but from a position of friendship.[1]

Mirroring Jesus's own unbridled affection, the Rahab workers live out the confounding reality of a God who, ignoring self-interest, takes on flesh to be with Sinners, for Sinners.

This, the Scriptures seem to suggest, is the pattern for gospel living. And though it diverges quite radically from the way taught and practiced by so many of the Religious, like me, it is nonetheless the unlikely way Jesus loved the ones identified as Special Sinners.

If you are ready to love differently, read on.

# 1
. . . . .

# naptime revelations

Kayla had invited me over to sit on her couch and chat during the sacred naptime hour. Aware of how much I had savored my own kids' naps just a few short years ago as a chance to pause and regain some semblance of sanity, I felt honored by the generous gesture. These naptimes don't just grow on trees. After her two toddlers were mostly tucked away—with the occasional monkeyish reappearance for a glass of water or help finding a lost puzzle piece—my friend began to tell me about her neighbors.

Kayla, Chip, and their children live next to a lesbian couple who are raising a son and a daughter. The kids from next door have played at Kayla's house. The four parents chat between driveways. They take turns borrowing eggs and sugar.

Eventually, Kayla got down to the reason she'd invited me over. With a heap of humility, she confessed that, because of their theological convictions, she and her husband couldn't in good conscience celebrate and bless their neighbors' relationship. Specifically, Kayla and Chip were concerned about what message they would send their own children by expressing *affection* for their lesbian neighbors.

Her face crinkled up in consternation, Kayla got a little squirrelly as she finally confessed, "I just want to know what loving my neighbor looks like."

## Fear and Safety

Kayla's dilemma immediately felt like one of those stories Jesus told where the answer is entirely obvious—like pausing to help a guy who's gotten beat up by the side of the road—as long as I'm not one of the characters in the story, the one who's walking by on the sidewalk minding her own business, and just doesn't feel like getting her cute new clothes all bloody on that particular afternoon.

For instance, to a gay person, especially one lying bashed and bloodied in the ditch, the answer to Kayla's question is a no-brainer. The gay person knows that loving one's gay neighbor looks *identical* to loving one's straight neighbor. Most folks in the ditch know this intuitively. The colleague suffering a difficult divorce yearns to be embraced by friends with the same affection that his happily married peers enjoy. The Sunday school teacher at church who's been accused of indiscretion is desperate for the kindness extended to all the other un-accused Sunday school teachers. When Jesus identified which neighbors we were supposed to love well, his was never a paradigm of *reducing* the obvious number, but of *expanding* it. And on most levels, my curled up coffee-sipping friend understood this.

But for Kayla—and for many of us—the answer to the question about loving her neighbor *wasn't* a simple one. Specifically, I could see in Kayla's eyes that Jesus's gentle tug on her heart to love her neighbors was matched by an

14

equal pull in another direction. Kayla was *torn* because her Christian culture had given her mixed messages about "loving" her neighbors. I too was wrought, because I'd gotten the same memo.

On one hand, Kayla and I had both been groomed to live out the new commandment that Jesus had given his followers, which was to love others the way that he loved them. In fact, we'd both been practicing this self-giving love—within our social circle of young moms—for years. Though I was still operating at sort of an amateur level, Kayla was brilliant at loving these women.

On the other hand, we'd both been taught to keep a healthy distance from "the world." With roots in the holiness codes of Old Testament law, echoes of these injunctions ring even in New Testament passages exhorting Christians to keep from being "stained by the world." Though the original injunction to purity was meant to keep God's people from becoming so much like the world that we were no longer salt and light *in* it, our eventual sterile detachment would mock the divine intention. Rather than *propelling* our salty, light-bearing movement into the world, we've used "holiness" as a barrier to protect us *from* the world. Could this really have been the intention of a holy God who got down and dirty with us and then died a bloody death?

For all of her adult life, Kayla explained, she had in what could be called "good conscience" kept her distance from *the world*, just as she'd been instructed. As she came to know the person of Jesus more intimately though, keeping a safe distance from her neighbors began to make less and less sense. Specifically, she could no longer remember why she was steering clear of the world that, she had been promised as a child in vacation Bible school, "God *so* loved." Surely, she reasoned, the egg- and sugar-eating people next door were included in *that* world, the one God loved, and not the poisonous one from which we were all carefully keeping our distance. Yep, it was all pretty confusing.

On most days, when I'm not straining to think as purposefully as Kayla and I were that day in her living room, the false kind of holiness by which I get to separate myself from people whose behavior makes me uncomfortable does not bother me one little bit. In fact, I appreciate the convenient excuse not to get myself or my clothes dirty. Every inch I retreat increasingly soothes the anxiety I'd naturally feel around folks who don't behave the way the Religious would like. For example, while I feel very comfortable among those in most any Presbyterian USA–flavored church, small Christian liberal arts college, or Whole Foods grocery store in the country, I feel more anxious among those whose differences overshadow our similarities. I do not always know how to behave properly around those beloved of God who are enthusiastically devout Hindus, or high school dropouts, or accidentally unemployed mothers who use their welfare assistance stipend to buy 2-liter bottles of Coca Cola and Little Debbie snack cakes at the Dollar General (under my stern gaze).

The more Kayla and I continued to unpack the kind of love that Jesus lived out in the Gospels, the discrepancy between the way we loved strangers who were a lot like us—mainline Protestants, privileged students, and affluent young moms in our neighborhoods who are savvy bargain shoppers just like we are—and the way we didn't love those outside our comfortable demographic, became painfully apparent.

## You've Got to Meet Him

When one of her children squawked, Kayla stepped away briefly to try to persuade him to sleep. I wish I could have been helpful, but in these situations I'm simply not. I tend to become so fixated on fantasies like adhering the child to the floor or strapping him to the bedpost with neon duct tape that even though I know it is entirely inappropriate, I'm rendered useless. So I just sat and sipped and kept my sticky solutions to myself. And while Kayla was gone, in one snap second, a chapter of my own story was suddenly superimposed over, in, and throughout what Kayla had shared.

Ashley and I had been chattering across a tall cocktail table at a local book launch for our friend Enuma. While Ashley sipped wine and nibbled hors d'oeuvres, I got an inkling that she might be able to help me in this little quest I have to find the Rare Religious. When I told her I was searching for Christian folks who were *loving Sinners well*, she mentioned her friend Bernie Newton.

As she described him, his alma mater, and his other connections, he certainly had the "right" evangelical credentials in place to make me think a Christian of his ilk would condemn the behavior of those who didn't fit the straight and narrow mold. So if he was engaging with people on the edge, he surely must have some hidden agenda. He'd probably targeted them for soul-saving or behavior modification. Maybe both. When I heard he was a therapist with a local Christian practice, I was certain of it.

Then Ashley explained, "He's a regular at drag queen bingo."

Isn't that just the most fabulous and ironic sentence you've ever heard about a Christian therapist?

That is when I knew I had to meet this guy.

My relationship with Bernie began the way so many modern human relationships begin: I found him on Facebook.

Before I officially knew whether he would accept my friendship—but, really, what friend of drag queens would be too

snooty to accept the cyber-friendship of a random stranger?—
the only access I had to Bernie was his profile photo. And let
me just say that it did not disappoint. The pic showed Bernie,
dressed very casually in T-shirt and shorts, sitting on what
looked like a parade float draped in a banner that said "North
Carolina AIDS Alliance." He was surrounded by fabulously
colorful human beings, who appeared to be drag queens.
Bright eyes, broad smiles, dazzly outfits, arms extended, they
waved at what I imagined to be crowds of onlookers. And
while it's technically possible that Bernie and some friends
staged this whole show in his backyard, it's more likely they
were all in the city's annual Gay Pride parade.

Though Ashley had told me Bernie was a special guy, I
still felt very confused and anxious actually seeing this Fuller
Seminary graduate sitting on a vehicle, in a line of other
vehicles, in the Pride parade.

*Maybe he's new to Facebook and doesn't realize that
everyone can see his profile photo. Poor stupid guy.* This
was my first thought.

But since he was clearly younger than me, it hardly seemed
possible I could have a better grasp on social media than
he did.

Confounded, because I simply did not have a category for
someone who was rightly Religious allowing other Religious
Facebook users to see him consorting with those they'd peg
as Sinners, I began to wonder if I'd ever be willing to post a
similarly scandalous photo.

For just a moment, I imagined the odd possibility of me
sitting on the side of a float in the Pride parade.

On the one hand, it's the most logical place in the world
for me to be. Even though no one with a good grasp of the
English language would ever even use the word "flamboyant"
to describe a straight woman, I really am. If the jazzy purple

rhinestone combat boot fits, wear it. And I won't lie: I would feel completely at home on top of a big crazy rainbow float with hundreds of people finding me a bedazzling spectacle.

On the other hand, the thought absolutely terrifies me. It would be like tossing my evangelical-in-good-standing ID card into the fiery furnace. I felt anxious just imagining someone from my church seeing my sparkly self. And while I don't think anyone would care enough to confront me, they'd file it away in the old memory banks. They probably wouldn't demand my evangelical membership card—because there really aren't any cards—but my name would certainly be written on the naughty list in thick black Sharpie. I would, in the hearts and minds of those whose company I enjoy, be worth *less*.

This rumination, of course, was all Bernie's fault. His stupid Facebook photo made me face the uncomfortable truth about myself.

In the end, though, it's really not about Bernie or the queens or the imaginary response of whatever church member I've imagined shopping at Whole Foods. It may not even matter if Bernie is straight or gay. Either way, this strangely weird occasion caused me to see—in a new way—my own heart.

What becomes crystal clear as I examine my own reluctance to consort with Sinners is that I am driven, in ways I don't fully understand, by a desperate and very primal wish for acceptance and inclusion in my social group. In fact, the evidence seems to suggest that I value it *much* more than I value patterning my life after a guy named Jesus who was despised and rejected for consorting with Sinners.

As someone who has spent decades priding myself on how much I don't care about what people think of my mannish shoes or unbleached hair or ill-conceived piercings, the realization that I actually do care what others think of me has come as a devastating disappointment.

In a blink, as Kayla returned and dropped back onto her comfy couch, I was overwhelmed by the awareness that my motivations were terribly problematic for a professed follower of Jesus who, trusting his Father entirely, was fearlessly unmoved by others' opinions, either ill or enthusiastic, of him.

## The After-Party

Kayla picked back up where she left off by explaining to me that her neighbors had invited her and her husband to the after-party they were hosting following the Pride parade. I'm telling you, this event is a very big deal in my town. Conflicted, Kayla had found a very polite way to decline. And though it had been several months since the parade, Kayla was still troubled by her decision. She *wanted* to love her neighbors well, and avoiding them no longer seemed, to Kayla, like love.

Freshly aware of my own wily motivations, I ventured, "So, did you feel like going to the party meant that you were *condoning* their relationship?"

"Yeah," she mused, "I guess I did. Is that crazy?"

Kayla had no way of knowing that, in my mind, it was the very furthest thing from crazy. Propelled by my own fears, I found it entirely logical.

"Not crazy," I objected. "In fact, *entirely* understandable."

Without intending to mislead her, I accidentally used a tone that suggested I already had this whole thing figured out. I must also have used this tone previously, in public, to have given Kayla the idea to invite me over for the gay chat in the first place.

Knowing my own heart, and taking a stab at Kayla's, I ventured, "Were you worried the *guests* would assume you condoned the relationship?"

20

"Well, maybe a little bit," she offered. "But I think there's even something more to it."

"So," I continued, "Maybe you were afraid that people at your church—who wouldn't have been caught dead at the party—would *find out* that you'd gone and they'd assume that you condoned your neighbors' relationship? Was that what you were worried about?"

A light bulb burst into brightness right over Kayla's head. "Yeah, that's it. That's exactly it," she confirmed.

"Me too," I confessed. I felt a little relieved to know I wasn't alone. "And that's crazy, isn't it?"

I suddenly *knew* it was crazy, but just wanted confirmation from someone outside myself.

"Yeah . . ." Kayla agreed hesitantly. "I think it is."

"And," I continued, "as far as your kids go—and it's possible I could be very wrong on this one—I think that if you decide to love your neighbors the way you love everybody else, you'll be communicating to them that you *love people*, even ones who are different than you. And that's really not so bad."

"Yeah, I guess you're right," she conceded, in grateful resignation.

We were quiet for a bit as we both tried to process a pretty significant shift in the way we perceived the world. I use the singular "world" because the world that God loved, the one for which he gave his Son, surely *did* include Kayla's neighbors. The world we'd been warned to avoid, the dangerous poisonous one, was the world where *fear* ran the show. I made a quick mental note to steer clear of it.

· · · · ·

Sitting in that silence, I realized in a very fresh way why Jesus's friendships with prostitutes and tax collectors were so offensive to *good* Religious folks. Jesus's liberality in spending time among outsiders was despised by the folks who attended the same synagogue as his folks and studied under the same rabbis as he had and bought fish from the same families. It bothered them just as much as it would have bothered some of my friends to catch a glimpse of me at the Pride parade.

So, of course, feeling like a dorky fish out of water, I made a point of attending the next parade. And though I was still too anxious and self-concerned to wear my favorite rainbow socks—sadly, not joking on this one—I stood there, one plain-socked foot beside the other.

Baby steps.

# 2

• • • • •

# sloppy dog love

This past weekend my church's annual retreat was held at the beach, and after it concluded on Sunday afternoon, I rode home with three other women.

When we pulled up Jen's long wooded driveway, her two dogs went absolutely wild. The moment they saw our vehicle pull into the driveway, these two canines scrambled to press their wet noses against the farm fencing holding them at bay. Then they began tumbling over one another for the chance to welcome Jen home.

Ahhh . . . home sweet home.

Watching from inside the car, I hoped that whatever humans Jen encountered *inside* the house would be half as thrilled to see her as her dogs.

As Jen tugged her luggage from the trunk, I began to imagine my own imminent homecoming. I travel often enough that I can usually anticipate how it will go.

When I've been with a group over the weekend, one of my hosts will often send me off, by car or by airplane, saying,

"I'll bet everyone's going to be glad to see *you*!" They stress the *you*, as if possibly my family can't even function without me. Though I try not to let on, I'm keenly aware that this is far from true. My husband may actually be a better mom than me, since he seems to know, intuitively, what to do with poopy pants and deep, jagged splinters and other medical maladies that leave me baffled.

Typically, I'll answer with something like, "Well, if they're not playing video games, they'll be happy to see me." Then I'll laugh nervously, but the harmless comment gets me thinking about how everyone will respond when they notice I'm home this time. Sometimes, everyone is out of the house.

Perhaps my adventurous groom, Peter, and his sporty friend Don have forced six children into two canoes to travel down North Carolina's Eno River in frigid temperatures. As they are pelleted by icy cold splashes, one canoe is leaking and the trip is taking at least twice as long as anticipated. Though I wish I'd been the heroic mother called by cell phone to pick up the weeping children from a designated spot on the route where they'd been forced to evacuate, I wasn't. Instead, after traveling I'd come home to an empty house. An hour later, my miserable, soggy children stumbled angrily out of Traci's van and past my outstretched arms, giving me the evil eye as they slogged by. I can only assume they were ticked off at me for bringing them into such a cruel world.

This particular weekend, though, everyone was home when I grabbed my own overnight bag out of Ginny's trunk. In fact, Peter and the kids were scrambling to finish the regular Sunday routine of household chores before I got home. When I arrived forty-five minutes early, miserable children were sweeping and vacuuming and cleaning toilets. Had I anticipated my husband's thoughtfulness, I would have had Ginny drop me off a block away and killed time by visiting with neighbors for forty-five minutes. Instead, I walked right into the hornet's nest under the misguided delusion that *someone* would be glad to see me.

Clearly, I was out of luck. Possibly *today's* furious glares were because I was complicit—along with their brutal broom-wielding taskmaster—for the fact that they lived in a dwelling. When they only communicate with the stink eye, it can be so hard to tell.

I suddenly found myself wishing I'd broken my no-gifts-upon-return policy that I'd instituted when my kids were toddlers. When traveling, I'd decided early on, I wouldn't bring home presents to bribe them into demonstrating enthusiasm and excitement about my return. Sort of smugly, I'd find opportunities to let other parents, the ones buying overpriced toys and gifts in airport shops, know, "I *am* the present." That, of course, was when my children were happy to see me.

These days, they're more often sort of *angry* to see me.

Now, sitting alone in a recently vacuumed room, humbled, I am left to reevaluate the no-gifts policy. I mentally scroll through the reliable airport staples—city-engraved spoons, magnets, and shot glasses—and weigh the potential outcomes against the generally foul moods of my preadolescents. I eventually reach the hard conclusion that there's probably *nothing* I can ever buy or do or be to elicit any sort of response to rival either the natural enthusiasm for my presence when my kids were toddlers, or the slobbery welcome of Jen's dogs.


## Received

We long to be received. We long to be accepted *as we are*, whether or not we bear gifts and whether or not we sanction child labor. Jesus was onto this when he instructed us to love our neighbors the way we love ourselves (see Matt. 22:39).

I'll tell you how *I* want to be loved: I want someone to be genuinely interested in seeing me and listening to me. I want them to really want to know who I am. And once they know it, I want them to accept me, warts and all.

If it's not too much to ask, I want someone to *delight* in me. I want them to really enjoy being with me. I want to be able to trust someone with the ugly parts of myself.

Basically, I want someone whose enthusiasm for the mere sight of me causes them to jump all over me and goo me with wet, slobbery kisses.

In case it's not clear, I like to be with those who see me as big. I don't mean they think I'm a big star or superimportant. I mean that I want to be with people who recognize and celebrate and encourage the best parts of me. It's not that they don't know about my weaknesses. They do. But when we're together, when I get to see me through their eyes, I am reminded of the unique gifts and strengths and possibilities God has planted inside me.

I do not like being with someone who sees me as small, and I don't mean they find me dainty or petite in any way. I mean that when we're together it's clear that they notice and remember and are sort of disappointed by my foibles and faults. It's not that they aren't aware I have something to offer. I suppose they are. But when we're together, when I have to see me through their eyes, I become keenly aware of my weaknesses and shortcomings and failures.

To be seen as big is simply to be recognized as someone who is worth receiving.

I'll tell you who treats me like I'm big. My friends at Reality Ministries, friends with various disabilities, treat me as if I matter. If I haven't been around in a while and show up unannounced, these friends holler at me and hug me and pull on my sleeve all at the same time because they're so happy to see me. And though the loud chaos sometimes makes me want to stick a fork in my eye, they give me the beautiful gift of being received exactly how I am, warts and all.

Of course I realize that being treated like a celebrity is hardly a kingdom value. This is why I don't *demand* it the way I might otherwise like to. And yet the flip side—to warmly receive others, to treat others as if they matter, to delight in another, particularly the most unlikely—is most certainly the way Jesus behaved.

A love that is particularly Christian doesn't demand anyone be other than who they really are. Rather, it engages others exactly where they are. It receives others just as they are. It loves others exactly how they are.

In a world where we like people to get what they deserve, it is, quite frankly, a little surprising. Disarming. Even disorienting.

## Email Surprise

Sometime last year, some thoughtless relative with too much free time forwarded me one of those heartwarming emails that's already been forwarded seventy-three times. Though I typically delete these life-suckers as quickly as possible, I accidentally read this one, and though I'm a skeptic about these emails, my research actually led me to believe that this one was the real deal.

Though "American football" and "gracious receiving" feel a little oxymoronic, this particular game turns out to be a crisp snapshot of what it looks like to receive others without any condition whatsoever.

> There was an unusual high school football game played in Grapevine, Texas. The game was between Grapevine Faith Academy and the Gainesville State School. Faith is

a Christian school and Gainesville State School is located within a maximum security correction facility.

Gainesville State School has 14 players. They play every game on the road. Their record was 0-8. They've only scored twice. Their 14 players are teenagers who have been convicted of crimes ranging from drugs to assault to robbery. Most had families who had disowned them. They wore outdated, used shoulder pads and helmets.

Faith Academy was 7-2. They had 70 players, 11 coaches, and the latest equipment.

Chris Hogan, the head coach at Faith Academy, knew the Gainesville team would have no fans and it would be no contest, so he thought, "What if half of our fans and half of our cheerleaders, for one night only, cheered for the other team?" He sent out an email to the faithful asking them to do just that. "Here's the message I want you to send," Hogan wrote. "You're just as valuable as any other person on the planet."

Some folks were confused and thought he was nuts. One player said, "Coach, why are we doing this?" Hogan said, "Imagine you don't have a home life, no one to love you, no one pulling for you. Imagine that everyone pretty much had given up on you. Now, imagine what it would feel like and mean to you for hundreds of people to suddenly believe in you."

The idea took root. On the night of the game, imagine the surprise of those 14 players when they took the field and there was a banner the cheerleaders had made for them to crash through. The visitors' stands were full. The cheerleaders were leading cheers for them. The fans were calling them by their names. Isaiah, the quarterback-middle linebacker, said, "I never in my life thought I would hear parents cheering to tackle and hit their kid. Most of the time, when we come out, people are afraid of us. You can see it in their eyes, but these people are yelling for us. They knew our names."

Faith won, but after the game the teams gathered at the 50-yard line to pray. That's when Isaiah, the teenage convict-quarterback, surprised everybody and asked if he could pray. He prayed, "Lord, I don't know what just happened so I don't know how or who to say thank you to, but I never knew there were so many people in the world who cared about us." On the way back to the bus under guard, each one of the players was handed a burger, fries, a coke, candy, a Bible, and an encouraging letter from the players from Faith Academy.[1]

Amen, right?

Whether sinful or saintly, the deep longing of each heart is to be received with abandon, regardless of who we are, where we've been, or what we've done. And with no more conditions for acceptance than a slobbery puppy might demand, Jesus does that very thing. And like a forward-thinking coach, he invites us to join him in making real God's kingdom on earth like it is in heaven.

To be fully received is the primal longing of every weekend-retreater and away-from-home teenage boy and work-traveling parent who longs for home. And though the reality for most of us is that the "home" to which we turn and return may not ever be fully equipped and able and prepared to receive us—certainly not the way a rambunctious dog or perky cheerleader might—the deep wish of our hearts remain.

Despite the inadequacy of human faces to receive us completely, exactly as we are and not as we should be, despite their inability to meet our needs and desires, we continue to turn our gazes toward them in search of the Face who does not fail.

Henri Nouwen recognized the futility of our habitual, almost addictive, search for human faces to meet the deepest need of our hearts. "The sadness," he muses, "is that you perceive their necessary withdrawal as a rejection of you instead of as a call to return home and discover there your true belovedness."[2]

Go home.

# 3

• • • • •

# internal consistency and secrets for manipulating people

I was excited to be back in North Jersey, where I'd lived and worked right out of seminary. As I dropped my luggage on the floor of a friend's guest bedroom, my eyes fell upon the single book that sat next to the family's computer: *Get Anyone to Do Anything: Never Feel Powerless Again—With Psychological Secrets to Control and Influence Any Situation* by David Lieberman. I quickly looked away.

As I unpacked my things though, my mind kept chewing on why my friend would be harboring this kind of literature. She worked in an office, but not in sales. She was kind, sweet, and accommodating. She wasn't the least bit bossy. And even if, in the secret depths of her heart, she wanted to control situations, she had the good common decency to hide the fact, like the rest of us. I did not know her husband as well. Though he seemed like a decent sort, maybe he was a cutthroat businessman who'd studied up on the art of manipulation. I couldn't know for sure.

After brushing my teeth, inserting my rubbery mouth guard, and sliding into a cozy T-shirt, I cuddled into bed. When I finished reviewing the presentation I was scheduled to deliver the next day, I slipped quickly out of bed, grabbed the book, and quickly popped back into my fluffy cocoon.

Self-conscious, I considered locking the door, but I was too warm and lazy. I decided that if I heard anyone in the hallway I could easily slide the book under the sheets. Then it would only get weird if the person had come creeping down the hallway and into my bedroom for the express purpose of searching for the book.

For having such a horrible title, the book was awesome. I enjoyed it so thoroughly, I believe, because Lieberman really understands how people tick. For instance, when he's describing how I might convince someone to agree with me, he frames the conversation as "effective persuasion." When he's helping me develop skills to *avoid* being persuaded, he calls it "avoiding manipulation." See? Genius!

The next morning I asked my friend about the book. Wide-eyed, she purported to have been as surprised as I that the content, in light of the dubious title, was so riveting. I asked if I could take the book home with me and send it back to her in the mail. As it had already been designated a guest room book anyway, she was happy enough to oblige.

With spine and cover carefully concealed, I continued to devour the paperback on the airplane. Uncharacteristically prompt about sending it back once I finished it, I later wanted to review the information. My Amazon purchase of my own copy is why the selections in my Suggested Readings email now read:

*Never Be Lied to Again: How to Get the Truth in 5 Minutes or Less In Any Conversation or Situation*

*The 48 Laws of Power*
*The 33 Strategies of War*

Thankfully it's not like Facebook, where this kind of nonsense is published for the benefit of all of my friends and random acquaintances. So far, on Amazon, no one is broadcasting these titles. Yet.

## Logical Consistency

Among the many wise nuggets in the book, one shimmered in my mind above the rest. The insight to which I found myself returning again and again was about something Lieberman called the law of internal consistency. Though he didn't make a big deal of it, he explained, "People have an inherent need to perform in a manner consistent with *how they see themselves* and with how they think others perceive them."[1]

How we see ourselves moves us in ways we don't even realize.

Not knowing whether the law was original to Lieberman, I searched a little online and discovered that understanding and utilizing this law of internal consistency is useful for automobile salespeople and is also handy when it comes to practical metaphysics for warlocks. So it seems like maybe everybody knew about this before I did.

People want to behave in a manner that's consistent with their self-image. So employing this knowledge persuasively is pretty simple. For instance, if I want you to share a piece of the chocolate cake that's sitting on your counter, I might say, "You've always impressed me with your willingness to share homemade cake."

Or I might affirm, "I know you're the kind of person who's not afraid to share a tasty, chocolaty delight with a friend sitting at her kitchen table."

Or I might reflect, "I've always liked the fact that you pump me full of carbs whenever I come to visit you."

Now, I don't think I actually would say any of those things, but if I did, my friend would be more likely to offer me a piece of cake, because giving me the cake would match a recent positive perception she has of herself.

To illustrate this, Lieberman cites a 1996 study by Freedman and Fraser, who asked homeowners to let them place a huge DRIVE CAREFULLY sign in their yards. As you might imagine, only a slim 17 percent agreed to allowing such a monstrosity to be planted prominently on their property. Other residents, though, had been approached previously to place a teeny tiny three-inch BE A SAFE DRIVER sign in their windows. Nearly all had agreed. And when this second group was asked to place the obnoxiously large sign in their yards, 76 percent agreed! Lieberman explains, "When we take a small step in one direction we are driven to maintain a sense of consistency by agreeing to larger requests."[2]

"I'm so thirsty. Could I get a glass of water?"

"Sure . . . want ice in that? Here you go."

"Mmm . . . thanks. Any chance I could have a slice of that cake?"

Now my chances of getting that cake are even better.

Perhaps right now you're thinking, *Unless we're talking about chocolate gluttony, Margot, I hardly see how your Jedi mind tricks relate to loving Sinners.*

All I'm trying to say is that we all like to see ourselves as a certain *type* of person.

For example, I like to see myself as someone who is a lover of underprivileged urban youth. As a result of this self-perception, I am far too easily persuaded to buy overpriced magazines from a teenager on my porch who tells me he's saving for an education. Because I've already decided that I'm *that* kind of person.

I also like to see myself as a person who trusts God. So when I waste money—buying craft supplies that I really want, or shoes that I might one day need, or Gatorade that I'd really enjoy—I can convince myself later, if not right on the spot, that my loose habits with money spring from an unwavering confidence in God to provide for all my needs. The fact that I don't ever budget or write little numbers in checkbooks or even deposit paychecks in regular intervals doesn't mean I'm lazy. It means that I trust God to meet all my needs. Because I'm *that* kind of person.

In case you're still not clear how this works, I invite you inside my head for a private tour.

## Trustworthy

First, know that I like to see myself as a trustworthy person. As a matter of fact, I humbly pride myself on it. So although I peeked at the private information being scribbled on a legal pad by the older gentleman one row ahead of me on a flight to Nashville, I, of course, still wanted to continue to think of myself as someone who doesn't snoop in other people's business. Since I wasn't *that* kind of person. By the time my flight landed twenty minutes later I'd succeeded, thanks to an intricate internal litany.

It sounded something like this:

1. How unfortunate for that man that airlines cram so many seats together. Those horrible airlines. It's just not right!
2. Corporations are so greedy these days, with the tight seats.
3. People who are just trying to fly places to see their friends, and are forced to see things they don't want to see, are the ones who end up paying the price.

4. Writing on paper, on an airplane tray, is really a type of public space, like holiday fireworks or an outdoor concert in the park might be.
5. A pad of paper on an airplane is actually sort of like a subway billboard that lots of people read.
6. The fact that I "accidentally" saw the name of a professional colleague of mine on that legal pad makes me the kind of person who's a pretty keen and alert noticer of details.
7. The fact that I knew the guy whose name was on the paper also probably means that I have an extensive social network.
8. That I continued to snoop long enough to assemble enough information to determine that I was seated catty-corner from a headhunter doesn't make me a snooping person, it makes me a very, very clever person.
9. I'm so glad I've never been one of those people who reads other people's diaries.
10. In the future, I won't be a mom that reads my children's diaries. If they ever learn to write. Because I'm not that kind of person.

By the time we landed in Nashville, I had effectively convinced myself that I was nothing if not an alert, curious, popular, clever, honest, and trustworthy person.

And all because I snooped.

## And Furthermore

The law of internal consistency means that we will behave in a manner consistent to how we like to see ourselves and, even when we don't, we—clearly!—convince ourselves that we do.

I tell you: we're a mess, people.

This law of internal consistency can be taken one step further. If we're people of faith who claim to be transformed more and more into the likeness of our God, then we need to find similarities between us and the Almighty.

There's nothing wrong with this. It's part of the plan. In fact, ideally, all of our ugliness and selfishness and anxiety and bitterness would be transformed so that our lives did conform more neatly to the character of the One whom we worship. In the event that this doesn't happen, though, we are still driven toward coherence between what we say and who we actually are, and we do this weird thing where we sculpt God into our very own image.

Author Anne Lamott confirms, "You can safely assume you've created God in your own image when it turns out that God hates all the same people you do."[3]

So true. And funny. Until it's not.


## Wisdom from Brother Charles

One fellow, I'll call him Brother Charles, is pretty convinced that Jesus was not a friend of Sinners. Of all the things to really put a stake in the ground about, this is it, apparently.

Brother Charles insists of Jesus, "He was not gluttonous. He was not a winebibber. He was not a friend of publicans and Sinners." The logic, here, is that Jesus's enemies only *said* he was a friend of Sinners because they were slandering him. That's how the whole nasty rumor got started in the first place. Since they'd spit out "glutton," "drunkard," and "friend of Sinners" in one angry breath, the reasoning goes that *none* of these could be true. Which, to my ear, sounds a little like the funny logic employed by that little Sicilian devil Vizzini in *The Princess Bride* when he's playing the drinking game with the man in black.

I'm not going to lie: people who use words like *winebibber* and *publican* sort of rub me the wrong way. In my experience, no good ever comes of throwing these words around.

Brother Charles implores, "Stop using the Lord and false testimony about him as an excuse for your wickedness and your evil ways and your love of the world. Just face the fact that you love the world. That's why you want to be around Sinners."

Brother Charles queries, "Do you know why Sinners don't hang out at my house, don't want to be around me—all that much—except ones that are seeking the Lord?" I actually think I do. But his reason is different than the one I was thinking: "Because we have nothing in common. I'm not going to sit down and watch sports with them. Or watch entertainment or play video games or any of this kind of worldliness. I'm going to talk about Jesus. I'm gonna pray. We're gonna go witness. We're going to do things. We're gonna feed people. These are things they will not do."

Actually, I'm not sure where he got his data about Sinners not praying or witnessing or doing things or feeding people. In my experience, Sinners actually do a lot of the things Brother Charles insists they don't.

"The reason they get along with you is not because you're some 'in touch' Christian," he explains, "it's because you're not a Christian at all."

Per Brother Charles's logic, Jesus probably wasn't a Christian either.

Brother Charles continues, "Be not deceived. Don't think you can go hang out with these people, and be among Sinners, and call yourself a friend of Sinners. Evil communications corrupt good manners. You *will* be corrupted. Sin is like a disease, an illness. When you go around those that are infected, then you become infected as well. It's not the other way around."

38

I had not wanted to believe that breathing the same air as disreputable Sinners might cause me harm but, according to Brother Charles, it seems like it might.

"Also, by being around those Sinners, and hanging out with them, and fellowshiping with them," he adds, clearly on a roll, "what you are doing is emboldening them in their sins. Because they will think, 'If this is really wicked and worldly, the Christian wouldn't be here with us.' If you weren't there, they might have repented and got saved."[4]

Absolutely dizzying logic.

This way, though, Brother Charles and I can think of ourselves as the kind of people who want other people to get saved by God, and still have nothing to do with those dirty, infectious Sinners.

Win-win!

# 4

• • • • •

# when the church plays
# weird theological twister

A few days ago I was delighted to receive an email with a subject line heralding "This Week's Pornography Convention in LA."

I know, I know, I should have been furrowing my brow in disgust that this debauchery even existed, and be irate that someone had sent it to me, and furious that—as I was multitasking between email and writing and editing—my lazy spam filter wasn't even doing its *only* job. The reason I wasn't miffed, though, was because I recognized the sender as my friend Anny. Recently I have come to trust Anny, blindly, on all matters relating to the adult entertainment industry. So, knowing that there had to be some perfectly good reason for me to be up to speed on what was happening in the world of retail porn, I smiled at this otherwise disconcerting subject line.

Anny and I had met last fall under the most unlikely of circumstances.

## Oxymoronicism

In late summer, apparently dissatisfied with the low number of civic and religious holidays in his Hallmark pocket calendar, Pastor Terry Jones, leader of Gainesville's Dove World Outreach Center, posted a Facebook page naming September 11 as "Burn a Koran Day."

Like so many others, I reacted strongly to Pastor Jones's suggestion. One of my reasons—on a very, very long list— was that, by virtue of the moniker of his Outreach Center, he'd dragged the Holy Spirit into it. The sheer absurdity of the word *dove* modifying the kind of "world outreach" this guy was doing kept me awake at night. In fact, such lunacy rekindled my longtime yearning for the Word Police to establish a theological task force to crack down on just such oxymoronic nonsense.

In the press, this spicy combination of the salacious and the ridiculous only resulted in Jones being granted larger and larger platforms from which to spout his toxic message. And even though everyone knew he was one Koran short of a full library, it was reported that his unbounded vitriol actually endangered American troops abroad.

As August rolled into September, I still hadn't actually heard Jones's diatribe firsthand. In order to continue fancying myself a thinking sophisticate, and not one of the knee-jerk reactionary types whom I so clearly despised, I knew I was going to have to listen to what Jones had to say. *Perhaps*, I mused, *there is a really good reason for burning the holy writ of our predominantly peace-loving neighbors that I don't even* know *about. I'll try to keep an open mind.*

However, hearing out this poison-tongued pastor was even harder than I expected. In fact, watching an online video of Jones being questioned by a thoughtful national news correspondent was the emotional equivalent of swallowing razor blades and then gulping a rubbing alcohol chaser. Though his explanation was not entirely coherent, I got the general impression that we good American Christians were just fed up with every Muslim person for . . . existing.

Convinced I'd fulfilled my civic obligation when I clicked "play," I experienced a growing wave of relief as the little minute-marker inched closer and closer to the end of the video. As it concluded, my gaze inadvertently fell to the teaser links that appear at the end of these stories—links advertisers were banking on that I'd click.

If you liked *that* nonsense, why don't you check out *these* related atrocities . . .

I'm always a sucker for this ploy. When the thumbnail image I'm supposed to click on features bikini-clad women carrying picket signs, it is highly unlikely that I'm not going to click. Though I realize that I'm not, technically, the target audience for these lures, I was itchy for any mental bytes to distract from what I'd just experienced, so I clicked.

## New Beginnings

Apparently, a church called New Beginnings Ministries in Warsaw, Ohio, had been picketing a local strip club. For four years, members of the church had shown up with picket signs in the parking lot of the Fox Hole on Friday and Saturday nights, trying to dissuade customers from patronizing the joint. Though this kind of religious outcry at debauchery happens at lots of places, the reaction of those who worked at the Fox Hole was different than most.

Specifically, the manager and the dancers at the club, fed up with the religious hindrance, started picketing the *church*.

43

On Sunday mornings they would set up lawn chairs outside the church's sanctuary, blast some music, and display their signs in order to draw attention to their cause.

Wearing their bikini tops and daisy dukes, the dancers held signs that said,

I have been misrepresented by people who don't know me.

Jesus loves the children of the world.

But I say to you, "Love your enemies. Bless them that curse you, do good to them that hate you, and pray for them which despitefully use you and persecute you." Matthew 5:44

Though four years of Friday night picketing by church members in the parking lot of the Fox Hole hadn't been so newsworthy, the Sunday morning picketing of a church by a strip club was a story newsworthy enough to be picked up by the national media. One pastor in Grand Rapids, Michigan, caught wind of this story in the news. When he mentioned it to his friend (and now mine) Anny Donewald, he didn't anticipate what would happen next.

## Holy Irony

Anny is founder of Eve's Angels, an outreach ministry to precious women involved in the adult entertainment industry in several of Michigan's cities. After learning about the conflict between the church and the strip club, Anny sat in her car, listening for God's leading. Silently, she implored of the Almighty, *I can't make out what you're saying to me. Please have someone call me so I'll know what you're saying.*

When her phone rang moments later, it was her friend Sheri Brown, who coleads JC's Girls, a similar ministry out of San Diego. Sherri had called Anny to dish about the picketing story that just had hit the national news. Anny knew immediately that God was telling her to go to Ohio. As quick as you can say *holy irony*, both women were bound for Warsaw.

When Anny and Sherri arrived in Ohio, they checked in to their hotel room and then drove their rental car, its trunk filled with goodies, to the strip club. There they had to wriggle past the protestors in the parking lot while juggling the goodies and boxes of pizza for the dancers of Fox Hole. Once inside, they got a table, shared some pizza with the women they met, offered them gift bags,[1] shared about their own lives, and assured the women, "God loves you, and we love you." For Sherri and Anny, pizza and goodies are about so much *more* than pizza and goodies. They're about relationship. Anny tells the women she meets in different clubs each week, "Anytime you want to hang out or need something, call me." The beautiful thing is, they often do.

Six women were working at the club that evening. Just two hours after Sherri and Anny darkened the doors of the Fox Hole, three of the dancers, who at one time in their lives had been followers of Christ, rededicated their lives to Jesus. Two others became Christians for the first time. Crazy, right? With Sherri and Anny, these women with few opportunities who were mostly moms trying to support their kids experienced being seen and heard, known and loved—unconditionally.

Admittedly counterintuitive, this unconditional acceptance—being loved before they changed even one tiny thing about their behavior—is what generated, in five women, fresh new spiritual beginnings.

This is what Anny and Sherri get to do every week. Partnering with other Christian women in Michigan and Southern California, they hang out at clubs, developing relationships with the dancers and with the management. They learn who the women are, what they are facing, and sometimes even what they dare to dream. Recently Anny and her crew discovered that one performer in Michigan, whose stage name was Eve, bred hybrid blue roses and aspired to be a botanist.

Recognizing the need for more comprehensive support systems, Anny dreams of establishing a housing and rehab center for women, like Eve, who want to leave the sex industry. This, in my mind, makes so much more sense than picketing. Coupled with pizza, it's pure genius.

## Matthew Four Sixteen

I have never been to a strip club. Although I know where one is located in my city, on most days I'm too afraid of public opinion to even make a U-turn in the parking lot. I think this is why I particularly admire gutsy women like Sherri and Anny, and the women who build relationships alongside them.

While I'm afraid to even *look* too long at one of these joints, Anny is no stranger to these clubs. For years she stripped in various cities, earning as much as six figures. During that time, Anny says, the Bible was wielded as a weapon against her. Well-meaning Christians, issuing dire warnings of damnation, begged her to stop. She calls what some of these zealous

46

believers do, especially among women who have already been physically and emotionally abused, a type of spiritual abuse. I can't disagree.

Anny's own radical conversion happened after the birth of her second child. It wasn't a carefully worded sandwich board sign that moved her, but rather strangely, it was a scriptural citation—book, chapter, and verse—that simply *landed* in her head. Without cracking open a Bible, Anny heard three words, "Matthew four sixteen," repeatedly knocking inside.

More than a little irritated, she asked her sister one day, "What is Matthew four sixteen?"

Her sister ventured, "It sounds like a Bible verse."

Anny's sister opened a Bible and read these words to her: "The people who sat in darkness have seen a great light. And for those who lived in the land where death casts its shadow, a light has shined" (NLT).

Anny knew she had heard from God. She spent the next three weeks reading the New Testament. Anny acknowledges, "I was radically converted." Devouring the Scriptures, Anny came to know Jesus personally. Wasn't that just so good of God? These days, whenever I stress out about finding just the right fancy, persuasive words to tell people about Jesus, or if I am tempted to hit a sinner forcefully over the head with a Bible in the hopes of drilling some sense into him or her, I just think about what God did for Anny, take a deep breath, and relax.

From this encounter with the Holy, Anny now assures the women she meets, "God isn't saying you're a whore. He isn't saying you're a home wrecker. He's not saying you're forgotten. He's not saying you're dirt." As might be imagined, her message is much more warmly received—by women who never once, as girls, dreamed that they'd grow up to strip—than the Bible-beating and dire threats of damnation.

## Not Quite Right

Like my sons pretzeled up in a game of Twister on the living room rug, the church today has pretzeled itself into an unwieldy theological position. Somehow we've gotten ourselves twisted up with LEFT FOOT BLUE on "We do not accept your behavior," while RIGHT HAND RED is reaching for "but God loves you and accepts you." Our awkward position, as gospel-bearers, is both theologically and practically unsustainable.

Some of us have done this because, wobbly, we don't know what to do with the given fact that a woman who has just experienced salvation through Jesus will most likely still return to her job at a strip club the following evening because the rent is due and her son needs money for a school field trip. This sort of situation makes many of us feel very anxious. To eliminate the discomfort of this kind of shaky ambiguity, we have planted one or two paws solidly in a posture of certainty: until folks clean up their acts, God won't accept them. While we're willing to entertain the ancient rarity that a dirty sinner like Zacchaeus experiences salvation through Christ, we do it with the clear caveat that the behavior we don't like ends *immediately*.

To be fair, transformation *is* Jesus's heart for these precious ones stuck between sin and a hard place. He expected that the woman who was caught in adultery would mend her ways. Before he released her to go home, take a warm shower, and have a good long cry, he made that clear. Jesus clearly had much higher aspirations for the daughter who'd been sprung free by the creative force of grace than the doomed gig she already had going.

Unlike Jesus, though, too many of us open our diatribes or pleas—via angry placards and hateful book-burning invitations—with "Sin no more." We want it clearly stated in the contract that the bad behavior needs to stop. Yet in the grace stories in which Jesus is the agent of transformation, he does it differently than we do. More often, he leads with kindness. Then, sometimes, as with the adulteress, Jesus wraps it up at the end with a firm invitation to transformation.

Let's be honest. *Strategically*, leading with "Sin no more" hasn't worked out so well for us. Giving these Sinners a good piece of our minds up front, letting them know how very unacceptable we find their behavior, has not proven to be as salvific as we'd hoped it might. Even the clever caveat of which we're so proud—"It's not *you* we judge and condemn, it's your *behavior*"—has not drawn any hearts toward the Father who welcomes the prodigal, the adulterer, and the lost before they (or we) ever clean up their acts.

The only way to spring free from our untenable contortion is to imitate Jesus by giving up our heel-digging posture of unacceptance. When we lift LEFT FOOT BLUE off of "we certainly do not accept you *or* your heathen behavior," we're finally freed to land squarely, with all our weight, on crucifix red: "In Jesus Christ, God welcomes Sinners who have not yet cleaned up their acts, and we do too."

RIGHT HAND RED
LEFT HAND RED
RIGHT FOOT RED
LEFT FOOT RED

I've met so many good Christians who've been waiting patiently for the divine spinner to rest right there: RED, RED, RED, RED. They know that Jesus didn't die for people who've got it all together, so their instinct has been to buy pizza for brazen Sinners, to get to know them, and to love them even when their lives are still a total mess. Many, like Anny, are already doing it. But, told to keep that left foot on blue, many more of us have been dutifully waiting for permission to express the Father's unbridled love and affection for these Sinners.

What we've failed to see is that the great cosmic spinner has already come to rest, once and for all, on the One who was graciously present among beloved Sinners, when he offered his blood for those who had not yet cleaned up anything about their acts.

And isn't that all the permission we need?

# 5

## viscerally repellant people who deserve the sour lemon face

When my friend's locks turned grey prematurely, her grade school– and middle school–aged children let her know, in no uncertain terms, that they did not approve. In addition, they made it quite clear she should get to work coloring it immediately. Their meddlesome criticism was all my friend needed to go to a thrift store, purchase a bouncy, bleach-blonde wig, and wear it one day when she drove her minivan through the carpool line after school. The looks of horror and mortification that registered on their little faces as she slowly pulled up to the spot where they stood were all she had hoped for.

Now, when I've tried to pull a little stunt like this, my brood has been neither surprised nor alarmed. On random days I've driven through the carpool line with a blonde Barbie wig, dressed like a gangsta rapper, or even dressed as a Christmas elf, and I can't elicit as much as a single jaw-drop. They're disgusted or annoyed or crabby in response, but we've long passed the point at which I could surprise them with my outlandish appearance.

Just once, though, I'd like to really knock their socks off. The closest I've gotten, in the carpool lane anyway, was to show up wearing makeup, a skirt, hose, and heels. Unfortunately, deducing that I could *only* be on my way to a speaking engagement, no one really freaked out. In fact, the only acknowledgment I even received as they clomped into the van was "Can we play video games while you're gone?"

No, what I'd really like, one day, is to knock their little socks off. I'd like to glide into the carpool lane with a fire juggler in one of the captain's chairs or a small circus elephant spilling out the hatchback. If I could just show up with Darth Vader riding shotgun or the Chicago Bears' Brian Urlacher holding my light blue carpool sign, I think I could really wow them.

And I'd so love to get that big reaction.

Rarely are we shocked, offended, or "up in arms" when we read about Jesus's encounters with folks in the Bible. Many of us who grew up in church were inoculated against these stories as children, and those of us who didn't aren't receiving any clues from Christians that we should be surprised, offended, convicted, or challenged by what we're hearing. We might be aware that folks around Jesus weren't *thrilled* with the company he was keeping, but removed by centuries, the particularities have mostly escaped us.

To our detriment, our experience of "the text" is decidedly different than the people who actually experienced the offense of Jesus firsthand.

Specifically, some of the debauchery committed by identified Sinners in the Bible, and Jesus's interactions with those Sinners, simply has not provoked us the way it did his first-century audience. Which, of course, is not to say that modern sin doesn't get on our last nerve.

It most certainly does.

## The Thieves

I've been robbed more often than I care to recall.

I don't mean I've been mugged. I've never been physically assaulted. Yet, for whatever reason, people of all ages, in various locations throughout the country and the planet, have felt perfectly free to help themselves to my stuff. Suspecting this may be related to me having too much stuff in the first place, I don't dwell much on the reasons I've been targeted.

In seventh grade, someone stole my brown penny loafers out of my gym locker. So that's like losing a pair of shoes *and* the two cents. The culprit also took my cool new blue Velcro wallet. (Unlike the shoes, there was no cash involved with the wallet.) The following day, when I went to the vice principal's office to report the theft, I couldn't help but notice that the student with whom he was already speaking was wearing *my shoes*. Though she denied it, he investigated further. In the end, the girl could not come up with a plausible reason why my bus pass was in "her" blue Velcro wallet. Wallet opened = case closed. Wallet and footwear returned.

In high school, a similarly shortsighted thief stole a sweatshirt my brother had given me. It was a grey sweatshirt bearing the name "Whitworth College," his school in Spokane, Washington. Certain that no thief from Illinois had ever heard of the school, I knew I'd identified my suspect when a girl wearing it passed me in the stairwell. It was the mid-80s and she'd ripped out the collar, like Jennifer Beals in *Flashdance*, and written all over it in Sharpie. I didn't even *want* it back.

When I left Illinois, crime continued to follow me. When I was a college student, a pickpocket stole my passport out of my backpack in South Africa. The year I graduated in Santa Barbara, California, a hardened criminal—or transportation-challenged adolescent—stole my bicycle out of my front yard. My only solace was that because I'd painted whimsical rainbow stripes on every possible surface of the bike, he or she had a lot of work to do in order to make it unrecognizable. A few years later, in North Carolina, a word-loving thief stole a Scrabble game off of my front porch. The only clue I'd find the next day was a lone "G" tile, halfway down the block.

Now that was low.

About six years ago, my husband and I came home at night to find a man in our carport. As if he'd stumbled upon a serendipitous garage sale bonanza where everything was marked down 100 percent, he was searching for just the right power tool. As we arrived, the man hopped the short brick wall beside the carport to leave via the lawn. As he began to scurry off, Peter tackled him. When that big bear hug became strangely uncomfortable, Peter loosened his grip, and the man wiggled out of his backpack and ran off. As the backpack fell to the ground, my husband's circular saw rolled out of it. And the burglar's prescription medication. With his name on it.

When we moved into our current home, thievery continued to plague my existence. Someone started stealing everything on our front porch that wasn't nailed down. Damp beach towels? Really? Ever since the porch-stealers took a wicker table and chairs, a recent gift given by my parents, I've had my eyes open for them. When our neighbors, eight houses down, had had *their* porch furniture stolen, they eventually noticed it being used in the living room across the street.

These thieving criminals are low, I tell you.

I now see how easy it is for reality cable television producers to find feature after feature for their *Stupid Criminals* series. I am toying with the idea of installing a hidden camera on my porch and pursuing a contract with some cable station to just broadcast live.

While these modern Sinners really get my juices flowing, I don't have the same visceral reaction to the kinds of Sinners

Jesus encountered. First-century tax collectors and ancient prostitutes have never given me one moment of trouble.

## Zacchaeus Was a Wee Little Man

In my first-grade Sunday school class, a piece of colorful cutout felt—a little smaller than all the other felt grown-ups—featured an unpopular little rascal named Zacchaeus who worked for the first-century IRS.

Felt-Zacchaeus's legs were permanently bent, as if he was sitting on an invisible chair. Adult hands would adhere him to a felt-tree on our classroom's pale blue felt-board, where felt-Jesus was already marching down the street through a big crowd of beige bathrobed people. Our teacher would explain that Zacchaeus's neighbors didn't like him one bit. This, I was told, was because his employment required him to collect their taxes, which were way too high. Some sentiments stand the test of time.

When felt-Zacchaeus was poised on his tree branch, parade-marching felt-Jesus paused as he passed to look up at him. Then, out of the blue, Jesus tells him to hurry up and get his butt down because he wanted to have lunch with him. He sort of said it as if they'd set it up on Google calendars weeks earlier and boneheaded Zacchaeus hadn't even thought to check his schedule for the day. Happy enough to do it, Zacchaeus scrambled down the tree to join him.

A lot of us *really* like this sweet story.

If we're short first-graders, gathered together on a piece of blue shag carpet, Jesus might as well be talking *right to tiny little us*.

If we are socially awkward middle schoolers, we might find it a little satisfying that someone friendless like us was finally getting a little respect.

If we're rich, we might kind of like it that—for once!—hippie Jesus who hung out with poor people showed some love to the rich guy.

If we have a thankless job, like auditing taxpayers or ticketing friends' cars, we might feel that, at last, someone recognizes our humanity.

If our own neighbors have ever given us the cold shoulder, we feel justified that they are *clearly* so dead wrong about us—since *Jesus* crossed people like them, who were angry and crabby, and instead chose to hang with someone sort of reviled, like us.

No matter who we are, we easily relate to this guy. We really like this story about Zacchaeus because, at last, the underdog comes out on top. Right? Or are we getting this all wrong?

## Sort of Different

Unfortunately, Zacchaeus *wasn't* the harmless social misfit we've cheerfully painted him to be. If historical accounts of first-century Roman tax collectors are to be believed, he was, rather, the scum of the earth.

Hear me: not only is he *not* the brainy lonely kid in the lunchroom, Zacchaeus isn't even the modern-day public defender in *Law and Order* reruns who is scorned for "just doing his job." It's not just that tax collectors were cursed with a stinky job no one else wanted to do, like cleaning out clogged septic systems. No, he was more like a modern-day human trafficker who used coercive power to profit from the labor of others. He was the 1 percent. He was a dirty, no-good traitor. A Jew, he pimped himself out to the Romans to extort money from households in his community.

A lot of money.

A tax collector was like a drug dealer who knowingly participates in the destruction of lives in his own community in order to make a buck. He's the cad working a Ponzi scheme who convinces an elderly couple to sign over their life savings right before he hops a plane to Club Mexico with their cash. He's the playground bully who slams a child against a recess fence until he hands over his lunch money.

I am telling you, these tax collectors were *bad* guys.

## Welcomed

There were various kinds of tax collectors too. The ones who collected customs taxes from passing travelers and merchants had to *bid* on the job and prepay the money to Rome. Then, while collecting taxes, they would extort more than that to make a profit.

Levi, sitting in his tax booth, might have been a customs agent like this.

Even though I always imagine a first-century "tax booth" being manned by Charlie Brown's entrepreneurial friend Lucy Van Pelt, it was really more like a *toll* booth.

When Jesus ambled up to one of these stands to chat with tax collector Levi, he might have attracted a few curious glances.

"Maybe," one observer might have said, "the rabbi is really gonna give it to that dirty leech this time! Maybe he'll remind him what his boy John the Baptist said to the tax collectors who came to get baptized by him, about not collecting more than what was prescribed for them. Maybe he'll really let those guys know how horribly wrong they are and that they better shape up or ship out!"

Except that's not what happened.

What Jesus actually said to Levi was, "Come here, bro. Let's hang out."

And that's exactly what Levi did. He left his booth and went with Jesus.

Jesus knew that this would not sit well with Religious folks. It irked the Pharisees and I'm sure it bothered most of the other respectable citizens as well. To them, Levi represented the riffraff who were to be avoided, not embraced.

Levi, though, hosted a large dinner for Jesus at his house. He invited the people he knew, including other tax collectors.

As I read this in the Gospels I have to remind myself that Levi wasn't a morally neutral party host. In his day, he was despicable and offensive. If the thieves in my life had known me as a neighbor, had grown up in the same Religious community, had robbed me eyeball to eyeball and then gotten away with it, I might be getting a little closer to understanding just how despised Levi was. Only then would I have the kind of visceral response to these criminals that Jesus's disciples and neighbors sure would have felt.

When I'm square in that angry mental space, I finally understand how Jesus's behavior around Sinners was so terribly offensive. In fact, I instinctively find myself making that face people make after they've eaten a sour lemon.

Glancing over at the countenance of Jesus, of course, I realize I'm alone on that one.

# 6

• • • • •

# little bit better
# than the other guy

As I fight my way through traffic, I like to imagine that car-butts are conversing with each other through their bumper stickers. For example, the lime green VW Beetle that announces "I brake for UFOs!" might be gently reassuring the awkward blue Chevy that apologetically announces "Just visiting this planet." Or a bright red scooter's naïve "Have a nice day" might be corrected by the conviction of a grey Honda minivan that "Lab animals *never* have a nice day."

I think you get the idea.

Just beyond the drop-off/pickup line at my kids' school is a traffic light that, for those leaving the line, is always red. Though it seems unlikely, improbable, and impossible, I promise you: it is never *not* red. The forced pause gives us all a little extra time to check out the bumper stickers on other parents' cars, conveniently allowing us to stereotype one another without ever having to get out of our vehicles.

Having played this little game for the last nine years, for me there aren't any surprises anymore. There won't be a fish emblem that doesn't have little Darwin legs and there won't be a slogan touting family values that's not facetious. What you will see are a lot of antiwar sentiments, rainbow stickers, celebration of midwives, and plugs for various environmental causes.

This morning I was stuck at two consecutive red lights behind a Prius bearing an unholy triumvirate of good will:

**What the public schools really need is a moment of SCIENCE.**

**Viva Evolution!**

**Minds are like parachutes. They only function when open.**

There was also a sticker on the rear window. Though it was curving around to the side in such a way that I couldn't read the whole thing, I made out the word "Institute" at the end. I could only guess that the first part might have been a hand with an extended middle finger pointing at the sky. And while I suspect that the driver and I might possibly agree on any number of things, it was the tone of the communication that left me a little unsettled.

This said, that Prius has hardly cornered the market on pretentious, condescending bumper stickers, because, of course, there are a number of equally unfortunate "Christian" ones as well. Since it's hardly helpful to list them all, and since you've probably seen your own selection, I won't try. Suffice to say, the general sentiment of some of these overly simplistic slogans is that we're in the club—and you're not.

Recently a guy my dad plays tennis with was wearing a shirt that said, "I'm American, Christian, heterosexual, pro-guns, and conservative—any questions?" Though my dad didn't have any lingering questions, he did promise the guy that he was going to get a shirt that said: "I'm Iranian, Jewish, homosexual, antiguns, and liberal." (Note to self: great Christmas gift for Dad.)

Sadly, this is too often the tone not only of our T-shirts and freeway car-butt monologues but also of the ranting we do among those of our own ilk. Rather than engaging in constructive dialogue, we essentially dismiss our opponents and their opinions as being worth *less*.

Though we'll deny it vehemently, we like to think we're a little better than the next Iranian Jewish homosexual antigun liberal guy.

## Worse at Hiding

Though most adults have become geniuses at hiding our biases, or at least denying them, kids are more transparent.

Our family had been watching the Olympic Games. Our daughter was about four years old at the time. After an inspiring gymnastic performance by one of America's most gifted athletes, little Zoe wandered off to perform some of her own moves in the kitchen. As she was busy doing her Olympic moves and flipping her hair, her brother, about twenty months old, waddled behind her shaking his toddler diaper-butt. During one break in the action, Zoe paused, for just a moment, to compare her own skills to the world-class gymnast we'd just witnessed on television. Taking a deep breath, she announced definitively, "I've got *way* more talent than that girl!"

To this day, the phrase remains a favorite around our household.

"I've got *way* more talent than that girl."

Now that Zoe's a little older, we enjoy another comically deluded soul: Kristen Wiig's ridiculous character Penelope on *Saturday Night Live*. Penelope is a narcissist on steroids. For example, when Penelope is invited to a party, she casually lets it slip that she's been invited to *lots* of parties. She's also familiar with *lots* of hors d'oeuvres. When another guest mentions they've known the hostess for six months, Penelope interjects that, since she's known her for seven years, she's probably better friends with the hostess than that other guest. When a guest compliments the home, Penelope emphatically announces that it's her favorite house ever. And while others try to control their tempers around Penelope's outlandish claims, inevitably someone will come completely unglued and blow a gasket.

In one skit, one of these new acquaintances explodes, "Hey, Penelope! Guess what? I have a cousin who lives in space, and I recently lost five hundred pounds, and you know what?! My wife and I got here by paddling a kayak down the street, and two minutes after my baby was born, she spoke *French*!"

Without missing a beat, totally emotionally unaware, Penelope coolly replies, "All I have to say is: I have *sixty* cousins who live in space and other dimensions . . . um, I just lost *seven hundred* pounds, and, um, I *invented* kayaks, and *invented* the streets, so, um, I have *six* babies now, who spoke forty-four languages before they came out of my stomach, um, and, uh, I can fly, so . . ."[1]

She's fantastic, right?

While I have no idea about Penelope's spiritual leanings, I can hear her prayer to whatever matron God of narcissists she might pray to: "Thank you, God, that I am so awesome, and a little bit better than that other guy over there. Thank you that I do everything awesomely. Always. So . . ."

## Not Like That Other Guy

A prayer that's not too far off Penelope's mark is a blessing that has formally been a part of the daily liturgy for prayer for Jewish men:

> Blessed are you, Hashem, King of the Universe, for not having made me a Gentile.
> Blessed are you, Hashem, King of the Universe, for not having made me a slave.
> Blessed are you, Hashem, King of the Universe, for not having made me a woman.

Though this blessing has taken various forms over the centuries—including my personal favorite rendering, "Thank you for not having made me an ignoramus"—some forms go back as far as the second century.

We hear this binary refrain in Psalms as well. The very first psalm sets up the blessedness of the one who delights in God's law and the doom of the wicked. Again and again, throughout the Old Testament, it's *us* against *them*. There were the bad guys and there were the good guys. The good guys were *us* and the bad guys were *them*. In some cases the distinction was one of ritual purity and impurity. Other times it was a matter of life and death.

Basically, this is how we are. It's not how *Jews* were. It's not even how *Pharisees* were. It's how *people* are. It's how we move through our world in every moment of every day, identifying with some and dissociating or disdaining others.

In the story that Jesus told about a righteous Pharisee thanking God for his rightness—"I've got *way* more righteousness than that tax collector"—and the cowering Sinner begging God for mercy, it's the second guy, says Jesus, who goes home justified. That Jesus suddenly does the rug-pull

63

move, tossing everyone up in the air like exploding popcorn kernels, turns our human way of being entirely inside out.

To our stubborn insistence that, "I've got way more talent than that girl," and "I lost seven hundred pounds, so I'm better than you," and "Thank God I'm not like _____," Jesus suggests that we might not be as different, or as special, or as good as we'd like to think we are.

It's reasonable to guess that pre-conversion Paul, a devout Jew, might have prayed something identical or similar to . . .

> Blessed are you, Hashem, King of the Universe, for not having made me a Gentile.
> Blessed are you, Hashem, King of the Universe, for not having made me a slave.
> Blessed are you, Hashem, King of the Universe, for not having made me a woman.

I guess there's no good reason to think that he wouldn't have said it after conversion too. He was still a Jew. He was still not a slave. And ancient literature gives no indication whatsoever that he underwent any kind of gender reassignment surgery.

After Paul's life is turned inside out, though—and he becomes as unrecognizable as you might guess that someone who was turned inside out might be—his understanding of the world does change. Though he still might legitimately bless God for blessing him first, Paul no longer strokes his own ego with this soothing liturgical assurance.

Rather, captured by the radical inside-out nature of Jesus, he turns the prayer itself inside out and upside down. To the foundling church in Galatia, Paul writes,

> There is neither Jew nor Gentile, neither slave nor free, nor is there male and female, for you are all one in Christ Jesus.

If you belong to Christ, then you are Abraham's seed, and heirs according to the promise. (Gal. 3:28–29)

Did you hear it? In Jesus Christ, he's claiming, every one of those distinctions that would make him, Paul, a little bit better than the next guy is entirely erased. To be Jew and not a Gentile, to be free and not a slave, to be male and not female—these things don't give him or anyone else a leg up anymore! What is *distinctly* Christian has nothing to do with our preferences, leanings, or life experience; rather it is our relationship with Christ (who doesn't note the distinctions we note) that makes us one people regardless of our differences.

# 7

• • • • •

# a fun party trick

My husband, two oldest children, and I had celebrated the second birthday of our youngest, Abhi, without him (and before we had officially adopted him), while he was still living in India. Though we enjoyed a yummy, chocolaty birthday cake, it would have been much sweeter to have him with us.

When Abhi turned three years old, he had been living under our Durham, North Carolina, roof for just over eleven months. So his third birthday needed to be a big blowout. And, indeed, it was a pretty happy celebration. We invited family and friends over to celebrate the life of our precious one.

Throughout the event, I asked guests to write something special that they loved about Abhi on a big sheet of white poster board. Dutifully, each one did. These affirmations ranged from the emotional, "He is good at expressing his feelings," to the social, "Abhi has a great heart," to the recreational, "He likes race cars," to the physical, "His thick black hair," and to the intellectual, "He is smart." Then, before he opened his presents, we read what had been written.

As I read them aloud to the crowd, I slowly began to recognize a fascinating pattern.

My five-year-old, who was sort of a girl genius, had been impressed with Abhi's intelligence.

My mother-in-law, with fabulous thick black hair, had admired Abhi's shiny mane.

My other three-year-old son, already headed for a career in extreme sports, noted Abhi's shared fondness for motor vehicles.

My amazingly kindhearted father-in-law, who spends all his free time helping people in need, had noticed Abhi's good heart.

And my husband, who at the time would let no feeling go unexpressed, had noticed and admired Abhi's lack of inhibition when it came to expressing all manner of emotions.

So . . . it was actually quite an interesting little study, right? I enthusiastically encourage you to give it a whirl at *your* next social gathering. The $20,000 question, of course, is whether or not any of it was actually true of my son. And I am delighted to report that every last word was true.

It's what we do. We are quick to recognize in others that part of them that resonates with who *we* are.

Had I strangely somehow coerced our party guests to use a Sharpie to transcribe what totally *bugged* them about the little birthday boy, I have no doubt that the results would be equally fabulously revealing.

## Weird Party Game

That would be an entirely different kind of party, right? While it's not the kind of fiesta I'd want to throw for my son, if you work in your company's HR department, it might be a fun way to recognize the special day of the co-worker who's given you the most grief.

In the morning, you could just text a quick invite to the office crew. "It's Joe's birthday! While he's out to lunch with his wife, everybody meet in the conference room and write something on the whiteboard that you can't stand about him. Come early to get your favorite color of dry erase marker." It might take a little coaxing, but once the office crew got going, they might really like it.

Joe can't take a joke.

Joe's too competitive.

He's all about himself.

Joe's a jerk.

Only at the end of Joe's horrible pre-party—hopefully before he gets back from lunch—does it come to light that everything everybody wrote is really about *them*.

Then, at the end of the day, they drive home all ticked off at you, the host, thinking angry thoughts such as: *What a jerk. I am totally not like that.*

## Method behind the Madness

I'm convinced that Jesus knows this trick. And though he would be way too classy to punk his co-workers at an office party, he wants us to see that this is how we are. He knows that, when given the smallest opportunity or by creating one for ourselves, we'll spend loads of energy letting Joe know just what a mess he was while never once realizing that we're ten times worse.

Not to mention in exactly the same ways.

"Why do you look at the speck of sawdust in your brother's eye," Jesus asks, "and pay no attention to the plank in your own eye?"

He knows just how enthusiastic we'd be to scribble Joe's speck of sin on a whiteboard in huge letters. Or let a stranger know how dead wrong he is in the comments section of a popular blog. Or announce another's wrongness with a bumper sticker on our car—every moment blinded by the log in our own eye.

> How can you say to your brother, "Let me take the speck out of your eye," when all the time there is a plank in your own eye? You hypocrite, first take the plank out of your own eye, and then you will see clearly to remove the speck from your brother's eye. (Matt. 7:4–5)

Though I think it's tempting to gloss over this passage, grudgingly admitting we probably shouldn't be as judgmental as we usually are, there's more there than a cursory slap on the wrist. Namely, there's the intimate relationship between speck and plank. Jesus didn't ask why we look at the eyelash in our brother's eye and pay no attention to the jousting lance in our own eye. He didn't ask us to take the marshmallow out of our own eye before trying to help our brother remove the microscopic piece of sand from his eye. He could have said any of those weird things. Except that . . . he *knows*. Specifically, he knows how we see. He knows that we don't see others any way *other* than through the specked lens of our own planky sin.

None of us see through completely clear lenses.

## Dog in the Fight

Sometimes history impacts our vision more than we realize.

Following World War II, when orphans' birth certificates were being stamped "illegitimate," concerned providers pushed for birth records to be sealed in order to protect adopted children from the shame of illegitimacy. Though this was initiated with the best of intentions, no one could yet foresee the ways that being kept from the truth would breed a shame of its own. Over the years the original purpose of the legislation, to benefit children, was forgotten. Gradually, the sealing of birth records began to be seen as an instrument to protect the privacy rights of birthmothers.

My friend Pam, in New Jersey, is an activist who works to change the laws sealing these records. When folks find out about the volunteer work Pam does, their responses are mixed, as one might expect. What's interesting, and not a little bit counterintuitive, is that, most often, folks who have no connection to adoption whatsoever *get it*. Those who can often trace their family trees back to the Mayflower and beyond understand, intuitively, why someone would want to know about their roots.

"Of course," they say. "Why *wouldn't* you want to know?"

Though it makes complete sense to some, there are actually a lot of folks who don't want adoptees to have access to these records. Those who are *more* reticent often turn out to be the ones with some connection to adoption. Adoptive parents, birth parents, and adoptees are more often the ones who don't share the gut conviction that every individual deserves to know where he or she came from. The reason is no mystery. It's because they have a dog in the fight. Specifically, they have something to lose.

An adoptive parent might fear he or she will lose the unique relationship they enjoy with a child. Though this rarely, if ever, happens, it's easy to understand how it could feel threatening. A birthparent who long ago sealed up this chapter of their life may anticipate emotional and social upheaval if their child by birth is allowed access to their identity. An adoptee like me, whose constructed identity has rested on *not* knowing, may fight fervently to deny others access to their own birth records in order to preserve their own sense of self.

My friend Pam shared with me, "At public hearings of legislative committees, it's fascinating to watch how the intensity of those who claim to oppose access for historical or 'legal' reasons outweighs the intensity of the adoptees, birth parents, and adoptive parents who are testifying that the original birth certificate belongs to the adopted person. Others not personally involved with adoption have noted this too and mentioned it to me."

My gut tells me that these relatively well-meaning lobbyists might be driven by the log they've got in their eye that they can't even see.


## Blurry Vision

When I lived in New Jersey, Janet, a single mom who'd adopted a son, had invited me to dinner one night to pick the brain of an adult who was adopted. After her sixteen-year-old son, Taylor, had gone to bed, she shared with me, privately, that she'd been in correspondence with his birthmother on and off over his lifetime. His birthmother had recently asked her to pass on a letter to him and Janet was trying to figure out the best way to handle it.

Though she hadn't mentioned it to them, she was certain that her family, deeply committed to Janet and Taylor, would be horrified about the prospect. In fact, other than me, Janet had discussed it only with a close group of girlfriends she'd known since college. They, she explained, had had some serious reservations about sharing the information with her son.

"Wait! Wait!" I interrupted, like a petulant child. "Let me try out my fun party trick!"

"Okay . . ." she answered hesitantly, not knowing where this was going.

I closed my eyes and concentrated really hard like the mystic I thought I was.

"Now don't tell me one thing about your college friends," I instructed.

"All right," she agreed.

Eyes still pressed shut, I announced, "I am going to just take a stab in the dark here." Then, like a bandana-headed fortune-teller, I divined, "One or more of your college friends has a connection to the adoption triangle. Either they are adopted, or they relinquished a child, or they are adoptive parents."

I opened my eyes wide for dramatic effect. Janet pondered the demographics of the group.

"Well, actually . . ." she began.

I could hear in her voice that I'd nailed it.

"BAM!" I exploded.

I didn't know if that's how real fortune-tellers wrap up a session, but it felt right.

Then I told Janet about the dog in the fight theory. I assured her that although my own radar is a little off-kilter, people with far fewer dogs in the fight than I find it natural, normal, and healthy to help a child know everything he can about his beginnings.

She seemed satisfied.

## Will Campbell

When we've got a dog in the fight, a plank in our eye, it's hard to see clearly. The question is: Do we ever *not* have a dog or a plank? I'm beginning to suspect it's unlikely.

To make matters worse, keeping those planks in our eyes *benefits* us in ways we may never notice or admit. Like first-aid

73

advice given for serious puncture wounds—i.e., a toothbrush in the trachea, an arrow in the foot, or a dagger in the gut—removing the plank threatens to do much more damage, to our self-image anyway, than allowing it to remain in place. So, either willfully or unaware, we leave it in place.

When the comic strip *Kudzu* debuted in 1981, Rev. Will Campbell was the director of religious life at the University of Mississippi. An author, preacher, activist, and teacher, Campbell was quite the colorful character. In the strip, editorial cartoonist Doug Marlette based the eccentric pastor Rev. Will B. Dunn on Campbell. And since Religious leaders are only found immortalized as nine-inch-high action figures in the rare high-end novelty shop, cartoon character Rev. Will B. Dunn is sort of the next best thing.

Born in Mississippi, Campbell attended Wake Forest University, Tulane University, and Yale Divinity School. A friend of Rev. Dr. Martin Luther King Jr., Campbell was the only white person present at the founding of the Southern Christian Leadership Conference in 1957. The same year he was also one of four people who accompanied the black students who integrated the public schools in Little Rock, Arkansas. The kind of person who lives out his values, a soldier of righteousness, Rev. Campbell really is my kind of Christian.

Campbell notes that although many of us would never dream of blanketing another class of people with unflattering racial or ethnic generalizations—publicly, anyway—when the class of people is *redneck*, even some of the most progressive minds and voices are complicit in ugly stereotyping. Many of us, liberals included, sort of *allow* ourselves this one satisfying inflammatory indulgence. Although I'm a Yankee, and was thus never taught in my home how or how not to use the word, my experience living in the South today confirms Campbell's thesis, that the word is used freely to mean not only "ignorant" and "backward," but more particularly "racist."

Campbell posits one reason why: "Is it because the larger culture, the allegedly urbane, sophisticated culture needs, and will find or create, someone upon whom to place the blame for our interminable racist society? We are not racist. They are the racists. Not government. Not commerce and industry. Not the media. Not the mainline churches. Not the academy. They, the rednecks, are the racists."[1]

It's terribly convenient, isn't it? Because if it's *them*, then it's not *us*.

Campbell certainly isn't saying these folks are innocent. "I hope you do not hear me simply romanticizing my redneck people. I am quite aware of our sins and failures. I know that many poor, rural, working-class Southerners joined the Klan, burned churches, lynched, beat little children . . . I know it well."[2] Campbell isn't letting these folks off the hook by any means. He just wants us to notice the ways that we've let *ourselves* off the hook. If it's the speck in their eye that's the real problem—or better yet, even if it's the gigantic redwood in their eye—then it's still not the plank in our eye.

If it's them [breathe deep sigh of relief here] then it's *not* us.

# 8

• • • • •

# friend-o'-sinners
# Jesus action figure

Though I wish I could say I'm a Sinner-loving savant, I'm not. In fact, more often than not, I'm one hot mess.

Typically when I'm with Sinners I just feel uncomfortable, smile awkwardly, and try not to touch one. If there is simply no way to avoid contact—clearly my preference—I try to act very purposefully casual. For instance, if I meet one on the street, I actually work pretty hard at contorting my face into a neutral expression that says, "I'm completely fine right now. Whoever you are, no matter what debauchery you might be committing or planning at this very moment, it does not rattle me one bit."

I'll usually dance around my palpable discomfort with idle chat about the weather or baseball or housing prices. And while I take a certain comfort in the laudable fact that I'm not slapping them in the face with my pocket-size lime-green faux leather Bible, I continue to find evidence suggesting that this awkward milquetoast way isn't anything close to how

Jesus interacted with identified Sinners.[1] In fact, I'm sure if it all came to light we'd find out that Sinners don't even enjoy my company that much, not with all my anxiety and intense straining to appear so doggedly nonchalant.

Because I am so anxious and uncomfortable around Sinners, I have, on occasion, conveniently shaped a Friend-O'-Sinners Jesus action figure into my own image. This way, when I imagine Jesus partying at Levi the Sinner's house, with Levi's Sinner friends, it's almost like I'm there myself.

If it sounds complicated, let me assure you that these funny mind tricks are quite necessary in order for me to reconcile my unbridled anxiety with the written biblical record that Jesus was physically *in attendance* at these blowouts. Since I'm so repressed I can't imagine Jesus cutting loose and actually *enjoying* the folks who attend these Sinner parties, I am forced to frame him, in my mind, as the campaigning politician who's seeking to capture the Sinner vote. This way Jesus sterilely, properly, and carefully attends these dinners as a calculated political move to connect with the tax-collector sector of voters. And I can really respect that sort of a go-getter.

And though I can visualize Jesus loosening his twine belt for an after-dinner photo op, at his stylist's firm instruction, I presume that he's probably not really *comfortable* among these folks who run in such diametrically different social circles than the one I've made up for him in my mind. (In case you were curious, I locate him in the snooty affluent suburbs of most any major American city, not entirely unlike the one in which I was raised and the others in which I have resided.) It comforts me to imagine that Jesus was as uncomfortable in these situations, the ones that we'd both just rather avoid, as I am.

Generously, though, I'm willing to concede that maybe he had *some* wine with his meal, if only to keep up the political ruse of being a regular Joe. Since I enjoy neither the flavor nor effects of alcohol, I'll bet he probably did what I do. He grudgingly swallowed a few sips—but not enough for anyone on the catering crew to force an unwanted refill—so that he could walk around nursing that last half-glass the rest of the night. Same with the food. Since savoring the sweet, spicy flavors could appear dangerously close to "condoning," he probably tossed it all right past his taste buds, dutifully choking it down.

What I'd most like to believe, however, is that after he'd won the trust of these outcasts through cautiously being among them, Jesus would gently confront a few of the guests about their bad behavior. If all went according to plan, each one of them would whiplash-repent, like Zacchaeus did in the middle of the Jesus-parade, confessing that the way they'd been living was totally wrong and praying the Sinner's Prayer. Then they'd make up whatever they'd stolen in quadruplicate.

But wait, it gets better. If, I tell myself, the dinner Levi threw in honor of Jesus was actually a huge farewell dinner to his professional colleagues, it becomes less like a *fun* party and more like a boring retirement dinner. I'll bet the majority of the party guests were already repentant and sorry about their sins. So Jesus isn't really consorting with *unrepentant* Sinners. And if any *pre*-repentant Sinners had furtively slipped past security, I'm sure it was only because they'd been so desperately driven to learn more of Christ and his message of salvation. Which I am graciously willing to allow.

These are some of the many ways I sometimes like to imagine that Jesus "partied."

The very last thing I, or my respectable friends, want to believe is that Jesus had any fun with authentic Sinners, or that he might not have actually gotten around to condemning them and their actions. The only possible way for someone like me to exegete and understand the clear witness of Scripture is to believe that the "party attendance" was only a disguise for a calculated evangelism outreach technique.

Believe it or not, it helps me sleep at night.

## Evidence

Unfortunately, the Bible itself offers very little support for my creative interpretation of what's sort of . . . plain. Two glaring facts exclude it.

One, Sinners *liked* Jesus. They hung out with him, listened to him, touched him and were touched by him, and threw parties for him. And while I can't be sure that Jesus didn't *eventually* address their behavior, I'm pretty confident that as the party was getting rolling, before the last fashionably late guest arrived, he wasn't cornering each entrant with a weighty, "Hi, I'm Jesus. I love you, but I just need to let you know where I stand on this behavior of yours: I disapprove. Honesty's the best policy, right?" Again, the convincing scientific evidence I have on this one, that he didn't lead this way, is that . . . they liked him.

If Jesus acted like a lot of us Religious act—standoffish and anxious and a little scowly and judgie, even though we're trying desperately to be purposefully neutral—he would have been at home alone on Thursday nights, not at the Sinner parties. If he really was as self-righteous as we'd like to make him, they'd be running *from* him, not to him. Instead, the clear New Testament witness is that these folks experienced being *received*, not rejected, by Jesus.

Two, religious people *didn't* like him. They accused Jesus of being a drunkard and a glutton precisely *because* he was surrounded by, and identified by, grimy Sinners. By association, Jesus *became* the outsider. If he really had been as squeaky clean, pretentious, and inhospitable as the action figure mold into which I've squeezed him, the Religious would have totally dug him.

Though I've scoured the Gospels in search of a Jesus who's just as anxious and uncomfortable and socially awkward as I am, I simply find no record of him there.

## Lost: In Translation

Remember that weird television show *LOST*? When a plane crashed on this random island of absurdity, people who had once lived normal, productive lives became trapped in a weird dimension where an endless parade of unwieldy threats jeopardized their personal safety.

At home on our couches and futons and recliners, we grew to love these friends. Identifying with those whose lives were a lot like our own, more than anything we longed for them to reconnect with their loved ones so that they could reconcile broken relationships or receive a longed-for embrace.

More than anything, we silently rooted for the lost to be found.

I am all about finding lost stuff.

Or maybe I should say that I apply myself to finding valuable stuff. When I bought a cheap metal detector, in hopes of finding lots of loose pocket change on the nearby college campus, I waved it over the grass for a while. When said wand produced nothing of value, I gave up.

Basically, the energy I exert looking for something that is lost is directly proportional to the value of the item I'm hoping to find.

For instance, if I lose a piece of lint off my sweater, I won't waste one moment of precious living looking for that lint. That fuzz is as good as dead to me.

If I've lost a pen or pencil, I'll look for a few seconds and then I'll grab another one from the bucket of writing utensils kept by the phone.

On the other hand, if I've been kicking a playground ball with my daughter around a 1.7-mile loop on a lush, grassy campus, and return home to find that, at some point on said loop, my keys fell out of my pocket into the grass, I'm going to go back and search for my keys. For the first mile or so, I'll ask walkers coming from the opposite direction if they've seen any keys. I'll fix my eyes on the path and also on the grassy edges we skirted on our clockwise adventure. On the second lap I'll kick my feet through leaves lining the side of the path. I'll wander in bumblebee circles through the three fields we cut through at the campus's corners. The next day I'll interview several of the groundskeepers as to the policies and procedures around found keys, trying to ignore their amused smiles that confirm my fears. I'll then go register the loss at the campus police station. And for the rest of my life I'll drag my feet through three grassy fields in the vain hope of finding these keys of great price.

The more valuable the lost item, the more willing I am to search high and low for it.

The way we use *lost* in religious parlance, though, can be a little fuzzy.

Sometimes, when we say someone is lost—which is something we Religious like to say about Sinners—we might mean that they're kind of "far gone." Our tone may suggest they're "hopelessly absent" or "beyond redemption." We might suggest that the wayward adult child who's addicted, or hooking, or imprisoned, is lost.

Oh sure, when we're really pushed on it, we'll admit that with God all things are possible. We'll reluctantly agree that Jesus can redeem the most unlikely Sinner. We'll concede that there's a one-in-a-gazillion chance that that person can come to a saving faith in Jesus and finally get their life turned around. More often, though, we might be tempted to put a comfortable distance between ourselves and those who are lost.

## Different Thing

I won't lie: that Jesus referred to people as *lost* really rubs my sophisticated twenty-first-century sensibilities the wrong way. Clearly, a lot of Jesus's insensitive language does.

For instance, when Jesus references "the poor," I want to take him aside and suggest that he might, instead, speak of "people who are materially under-resourced." Or when he tells a story about lepers, I'd much prefer he describe "men and women living with a debilitating neurological condition." Though I probably wouldn't ever have the guts to gently touch Jesus's arm and ask if we could speak in private, I'm sure I'd try to model some better language in conversation when it was my turn to speak.

My twenty-first-century sophistication really isn't helpful at all with the first-century text, because if I edited out every reference in the Gospels to sick girls, demon-possessed boys, bent and sinful and hemorrhaging women, blind and paralyzed and leprous men, there'd be little left.

So most days, I let it go.

It still chafes, though. Specifically, Jesus identifying people as *lost* had been sort of bothering me the way *Sinner* bothers me. It was bothering me because I was hearing *lost* through my irksome twenty-first-century filter, which makes it sound as though Jesus identified these precious individuals as being worth *less*.

What actually transpires in the Gospels, though, is the opposite of that.

The Religious leaders were bent out of shape about the company Jesus was keeping. Namely, they were disgusted that he welcomed and ate with folks they called Sinners. Though the sampling of sins was probably more diverse than the peek we're given, we know this motley crew included prostitutes and tax collectors. Perhaps gluttons and alcoholics too. And when the Religious folks called these people Sinners, their expression and tone and behavior did suggest that they were worth less.

Jesus, though, describes the value that his Father gives Sinners we call lost. Luke shares Jesus's telling of three of these stories in rapid-fire succession.

"When my dad brings home one of these lost ones, he is totally psyched! He hoists that one up on his shoulders and asks his friends to rejoice with him. Those who are lost are *this* precious to my father."

"One of these 'Sinners' who is lost is so beloved by my father that, when one gets away, he scours the house for her. And the finding of her is so significant, that—like a lady who finds her lost gold piece—God invites others to rejoice as well."

And just in case it wasn't already entirely clear, Jesus makes it plain.

"Even when the behavior of the lost is as *bad* as it gets— because blowing your dad's cash on raucous living is pretty bad—my father throws a party when the son who was lost finally limps home."

It's pretty clear that Jesus, by way of sharing these stories, doesn't equate *lost* and *Sinner* with "worthless." To the contrary, he would say they are "priceless."

## Another Notable Sinner

Jesus was on his way to Jerusalem when he passed through Jericho. And once again, caught publicly rubbing shoulders with Sinners, Jesus received the stink-eye from the fickle crowds who'd gathered in the street to see him. When Jesus reached the sycamore tree where short Zacchaeus—excuse me, a vertically challenged man—had climbed, he paused beneath it, and spoke.

"Get down here, Zach! I'm crashing at your place today."

Well, those gathered were none too pleased about this development. Everyone who'd witnessed it began to mutter, "He has gone to be the guest of a sinner" (Luke 19:7). From their perspective, either Jesus had poor judgment—like someone who foolishly picks up potentially dangerous hitchhikers—or he meant to identify publicly with a Sinner. It's clear that neither was palatable to the crowd.

After a sudden act of spontaneous repentance by Zacchaeus, Jesus explains to the crowd, "Hey guys, this wasn't accidental. It's not that my Sinner Radar is defective. In fact, it's working great, because this is *exactly* why I came: to seek and save the lost."

Yet again, the one the crowds called Sinner—aka worth *less*—was exactly the one Jesus identified as entirely worthy of his, and his Father's, time and attention. Honestly, it almost makes me want to be more lost than, on most days, I think I am.

## Confession of the Religious

If we are entirely honest, many of us Religious care *more* about behavior modification than we do about spiritual transformation. So though we can sing a mean praise chorus and flip to Psalm 23 *really* fast, some of us who want to believe we're very Christlike have failed miserably to pattern our lives after Jesus. Basically, a lot of us have no idea what to do with Sinners.

And yet a cursory peek at the Gospels suggests that the ethnically different, spiritually diverse, curious, brokenhearted, broken-bodied, excluded, and bad-smelling ones are precisely the ones toward whom Jesus would run today.

His compassionate witness is the consistent welcome of outsiders as they are. Entirely secure in the Father's love for him and for the world, Jesus engaged all manner of excluded others, notable Sinners and otherwise, with a flagrant disregard for cultural and religious boundaries.

Whether or not I am willing to do so remains to be seen.

# 9
• • • • • •
## who even knew about exclusive paganists?

"Who wants waffles?"

The birthday girl herself holds a tray of steaming hot waffles. When no one else responds, I grab an empty plate and stick it out.

"I'll have a waffle," I offer generously.

As it's hitting my plate, she quickly adds, "They're sweet potato waffles."

By the time I hear that the waffle has been tainted by an actual vegetable, there's not enough time to yank my plate away. Forcing a smile, I take it.

Tastiest waffle I've ever had.

After eating I wander outside, where two women are eating at a little table in the front yard. Happy to be away from the noise of all the indoor voices, I pause to chat with them.

"What are you working on?" one of the ladies asks.

I try to find a way to tell them what I'm doing without saying "Sinner."

"Well . . . I'm interested in how some in the church treat folks like . . . strippers, and those in the gay community, and even people who are divorcing, folks that the church might identify as . . . "

I pause, because I still don't want to say the word *Sinners*.

"*Others*," Kelli says, finishing the sentence for me.

I look a little surprised when she says it, because she's given voice to what I've not yet been able to articulate about this little adventure on which I find myself.

Others.

It's not that I haven't heard the word. My husband's been suggesting I think about it, and has even pieced together a requisite reading list. Suddenly, though, the term *other* seems very useful in relation to how we Religious behave in relation to those deemed as *Sinners*.

## Otherness

Dr. Lilia Melani teaches at the Brooklyn campus of CUNY. Succinctly, she describes the *other*:

> The Other is an individual who is perceived by the group as not belonging, as being different in some fundamental way. Any stranger becomes the Other. The group sees itself as the norm and judges those who do not meet that norm (that is, who are different in any way) as the Other. Perceived as lacking essential characteristics possessed by the group, the Other is almost always seen as a lesser or inferior being and is treated accordingly. The Other in a society may have few or no legal rights, may be characterized as less intelligent or as immoral, and may even be regarded as sub-human.[1]

She really hit the nail on the head. In fact, if we trade out just a few words, the result is painfully telling.

The Sinner is an individual who is perceived by the Religious as not belonging, as being different in some fundamental way. Any stranger becomes the Sinner. The Religious crowd sees itself as the norm and judges those who do not meet that norm (that is, who are different in any way) as a Sinner. Perceived as lacking essential characteristics possessed by the Religious, the Sinner is almost always seen as a lesser or inferior being and is treated accordingly. The Sinner in a society may have few or no legal rights, may be characterized as less intelligent or as immoral, and may even be regarded as sub-human.

These aren't Melani's exact words, of course. Nonetheless, the shoe fits. And it fits because, over centuries and across continents, the Religious do not have a stellar track record when it comes to loving the ones we've decided are *other* than us.

Recently the national retail chain Lowe's, following a conservative Christian group's call for businesses to boycott advertising on a new TLC reality show about Muslims, pulled its advertisements from *All-American Muslim*. The Florida Family Association (FFA) claims the series, which follows five families in and around Dearborn, Michigan, is nothing more than propaganda masking a radical Islamic agenda. Though the FFA suggests over sixty other advertisers have also pulled their ad dollars, these reports have not yet been confirmed. In any case, Lowe's has borne the brunt of media criticism for pulling their ads from the show.

The FFA's problem with *All-American Muslim* is that the Muslims being featured are not radical *enough*. One is a high school football coach. One is expecting her first child. Another goes shopping for the traditional *hijab* after abandoning it following September 11. With the exception of some items on their shopping lists, these folks feel pretty similar to most other middle-class Americans. But not according to FFA, which says "the show profiles only Muslims that appear to be ordinary folks while excluding many Islamic believers whose agenda poses a clear and present danger to the liberties and traditional values that the majority of Americans cherish."[2]

So their big beef is that Muslims aren't being stereotyped enough. Seriously, that's the issue. And the FFA's twisty logic is subtle, so don't miss it. By using the phrase "appear to be," FFA is not willing to admit that these Muslim Americans might actually *be* ordinary folks. Rather, to support the imaginary agenda—and to promote their own—the organization maintains that somehow, TLC producers are *tricking* us by presenting only those families who "appear" to be ordinary.

The group is right about one thing: *someone* is masking reality to promote a radical social agenda. I just don't think it's these families in Michigan. Appearing on ABC's *World News*, FFA founder David Caton insisted, "This program creates an image that's harmful, education-wise, to the beliefs, structure, and memories of millions of Americans who will look at this and say, 'Well, all Muslims are like that,' when it's not accurate."[3]

If you find Caton's statement confusing, you're not alone.

As a reality barometer, ask yourself if it would be *more* or *less* true to invert Caton's statement. Would it more true or less true to say, "Not all Muslims are radical extremists"? Sadly, Caton has distorted truth to suit his group's ends.

Ironically, to watch the show would mean being *educated*, in a rudimentary way, about what "they" are really like. And for groups like the FFA, that's very dangerous. The success of Caton's group, and others like it, depends on creating images of "the other" that are frightening and inherently distorted. When the Muslim community becomes our teacher—or the Mormon community, or the gay community, or the poor community—the stick-figure straw men that we *use*, and abuse, will be exposed.

## Wizards and Vampires

Recently, at Whole Foods, I had a similar opportunity to become a little better educated myself. Though I don't do all my grocery shopping there, I dip in occasionally for something special. When a friend fell ill last week, I stopped to pick up a meal. Since I barely have the skill to cook tasty carnivorous meals, there was no way I was going to test out my vegan skills on an ailing friend. Nothing about that whispers compassion.

At the checkout aisle, a magazine on the top rack caught my eye. It wasn't *Us* or *People* or *The Star*, like it might have been at my own lowbrow market, demanding my attention by flashing an emaciated picture of Angelina Jolie. No, this one was called *Pagans and Witches*. Honestly, who even knew these people had publications?

It was sort of like finding money on the street, because for a Religious like me, you just don't get any more *other* than pagans and witches. The fact that it was a stack of papers stapled together, and not a real person with feelings and opinions and a face and a voice, made it even seem almost manageable. Baby steps.

It took me about a week to gather up my courage to purchase one. Part of me just sort of wanted to embrace the challenge of doing it, and another part really wanted to imagine how God sees these folks and how I could love them.

Finally, one night I went into the store with the express purpose of buying the magazine. After grabbing a fresh garlic pizza, I crept over to the checkout aisle. There was really no need to creep, except that *I* knew I was looking for the magazine. Someone had moved the stack from the top shelf to the bottom shelf. Which, thankfully, made for a less conspicuous pickup. Bending over as if I had dropped something important, I snatched a magazine and held it

91

against my pizza. When the customer in front of me left, I dropped both items on the checkout conveyor belt, purposing not to look, like a teenage boy pretending he's *not* buying a *Playboy* magazine.

I wondered what the cashier thought about me buying this magazine. Though she probably had a hundred other things to noodle on, and was probably no more interested in my reading material than the cashier at the lowbrow grocery store would have been in my trashy tabloid literature, I kind of made it all about me. If the cashier were Religious, she might have felt as uncomfortable as I would have felt if a witch showed up at my workplace. If she were a witch, she might have looked me over and made a mental note to herself that now they're letting witches who wear too many polka dots and mismatched socks into the club. And if she were new to the store, I might have been the only witch-suspect she'd ever seen. For all she knew they might *all* wear polka dots. If she were not a Christian *or* a witch, she might have just been wondering, like me, what a modern "pagan" even *was*. These are the things I think about. Clearly, I cared very much about my cashier's opinion of me.

"Do you want a bag?"

Though what I really wanted was an armored truck, the words I heard myself say were, "No thanks, I'm good." If I'm on foot, I have a no-bag policy if I can shove all my goods into a backpack. When I'm driving a vehicle, the no-bag policy applies if I can stack up the items in my arms and carry them—teetering—to my vehicle. So I refused the bag on principle, before I realized how handy it would have been to hide my magazine from passersby.

Flipping it facedown on the pizza achieved the same end. Pressing both literature and pizza to my chest, I escaped to my vehicle.

## Anxious Browsing

When I got home and finally opened the magazine, I was a little nervous. Like maybe bats would whoosh out of the pages and haunt my house.

On the inside of the front cover was an ad for eight-inch resin statues of goddesses. Two beige figures, symbolic of the female figure, were displayed. The copy next to the statues read, "Invoke magic. Raise energy. Wield power. Invite creativity." It's not clear to me that there's a relationship between what's written and the actual statues, but I understand that this is pretty much how most advertising, pagan or otherwise, works.

Flipping through a few more pages of ads for services and products I didn't understand, I paused to read the letter from the editor, which included a conversation happening within the pagan culture.

In the context of a larger discussion, reference was made to the ways in which currently or formerly incarcerated individuals are treated within the pagan community. In a previous issue, apparently, one writer had implored, "It is high time we recognize that no one is perfect, and open at least some of our meetings, festivals, and our hearts to sincere ex-prisoner seekers who wish to be part of our communities."

So it was sort like I could have been reading a newsletter from Prison Fellowship.

Apparently, this comment generated quite a flood of letters in response. In one, a particularly salty fellow identified those who were incarcerated as "the useless societal waste that ends up in our various prison systems." He continued, "As far as I am concerned the rapists and child molesters should be rounded up and executed because they don't deserve to live on our planet. These [criminals] are useless pimples on the back side of our society, they deserve our contempt, not our compassion."

To be clear, I do not, for one second, blame his disconcerting views on paganism.

In the context of the piece, the two conflicting opinions were offered by the editor as examples of different perspectives within paganism. The editor herself acknowledged that she favored a "vigorous prisoner/ex-con ministry." She reasoned that with more professing pagans, heathens, and polytheists, there would be less *lost souls* roaming the planet.

For Christian readers, this is like the crazy tilting house of mirrors carnival ride, right?

Though I could certainly relate to "prison ministry," I was struck by the way in which the salty man we'd deem to be so radically *other*—possibly even outside the grasp of God's grace—had also deemed a *different* group to be so radically other that he considered them outside the grasp of the gods and goddesses.

So it's official: as a *race*, hell-bent on excluding the other, we are totally messed up.

## Theory of Relativity

If you've made it this far in the book, then you might be willing to consider implementing some of these ideas about moving toward the Sinners God loves. (If you accidentally got here by clicking "Surprise Me!" on Amazon, you might want to read a few more pages first. Then come back.) If you're up for an adventure, you might be willing to *touch* a *Pagans and Witches* magazine, or strike up a conversation with a girl who's pregnant out of wedlock, or dine with a glutton. Bravo. You'll probably meet some awesome Sinners.

But since Jesus calls each one of us to engage with those who are entirely *other*—the way he challenged righteous Pharisees to treat the unrighteous as human beings—keep thinking about who is diametrically *other* than you. Sure, for some of us the *other* will be a crack-smoking exotic dancer named Candy. And that will be awesome. Perhaps the other might just as easily be Rush Limbaugh. Or the relative of yours who so often seems to *channel* Mr. Limbaugh. Or maybe God will invite you to love your multimillionaire neighbor who can buy himself out of any sin he, or his loved ones, commit. Or maybe Jesus will invite you to love your law-abiding, rule-following racist neighbor.

If you're in favor of gay marriage, maybe God is calling you to know and love your neighbor whose *Focus on the Family* magazine accidentally ended up in your mailbox. If you're a pacifist, perhaps God will call you to love the retired United States Army general who didn't just *bear* war but *loved* it. If you work for Planned Parenthood, maybe you'll be invited to love your old high school classmate who is now a pro-life activist.

Since Sinners come in all shapes and sizes, just be sure not to let yourself off the hook too easily.

# 10
• • • • •

## three fingers pointing
## back at me

When first-century Religious leaders accused Jesus of being a glutton, I don't know exactly what *they* had in mind, but I know what *I* have in mind.

When I imagine a sinful glutton, I'm thinking of this pudgy, shifty-looking guy in Hieronymous Bosch's 1485 painting *The Seven Deadly Sins and the Four Last Things*. This fleshy character has a stein of beer in one hand and is gnawing on a meaty bone in the other hand. His clothing, bursting at the seams, can no longer contain his full belly. A hungry child at his feet holds out his hands for a morsel that does not come. If my culinary eye serves me well, the man is surrounded by platters of chicken, ham, beef, and pork. And if the platters weren't enough, on the floor of his dining room is a little campfire where he or his maidservant is alternately roasting a plump kielbasa and brewing something tasty in a kettle.

Though Bosch's painting doesn't include any of those handy little cartoon bubbles for dialogue, this repugnant character looks like he could be thinking something evil like, *If I had to choose between the life of my child, and sucking the marrow out of this turkey leg, I'd need awhile to think about it.*

Yes, this guy, I am certain, is a bona fide glutton. But as I do more research on exactly what a glutton is, I'm dismayed by what I find.

## Saint Gregory

Saint Gregory, who served as pope in the late sixth and early seventh centuries, was a prolific writer. Among his writings, Gregory described five ways in which the sin of gluttony is committed. Imagine my surprise when I not only recognized myself in Gregory's list, but discovered that his descriptors are actually an articulation of the current "operating procedures" I'm implementing with my eating practices right now.

Here are Gregory's criteria:

1. *Time*. Eating before the time of meals in order to satisfy the palate.
2. *Quality*. Seeking delicacies and better quality of food to gratify the "vile sense of taste."
3. *Stimulants*. Seeking after sauces and seasonings for the enjoyment of the palate.
4. *Quantity*. Exceeding the necessary amount of food.
5. *Eagerness*. Taking food with too much eagerness, even when eating the proper amount, and even if the food is not luxurious.

What was so intriguing about this list, of course, is how I purposefully *embrace* every single criteria he warns us to avoid.

1. *Time*. **Eating before the time of meals in order to satisfy the palate.**

Since I work from home, observing rigid mealtimes makes less sense for me than it does for someone like my daughter, whose 12:43 lunch period is scheduled into her school day routine. And if I'm to believe nutritionists on this subject, what I've got going—nibbling pretzels at 9:30, sucking a Now and Later at 10:15 (and then maybe again . . . later), then gulping down a dish of cottage cheese, applesauce, and raisins at 11:30, and maybe a cookie at 11:45—is actually *healthier* than eating just three big meals. This is what they say these days. And, of course, Saint Greg had no way of knowing about modern nutritional research.

I'll confess that while it doesn't take a lot of caloric energy to perform my work functions, as I sit mostly motionless while wiggling my fingers on a keyboard, eating before mealtimes has been scientifically proven to be a healthy option.

2. *Quality*. **Seeking delicacies and better quality of food to gratify the "vile sense of taste."**

While I will be the first to admit that I do not have a very refined palate, I am nonetheless all about taste. So while, when invited to a New Year's Eve party, I'd rather find bowls of Cheetos and M&Ms scattered on coffee tables and end tables than white-shirted servers passing caviar and fancy foie gras, it's still a matter of gratifying my vile sense of taste. It just turns out that my lowbrow tastes are more financially feasible for me than for those with a penchant for actual delicacies.

3. *Stimulants*. **Seeking after sauces and seasonings for the enjoyment of the palate.**

Stimulant seeking? Guilty. This apparent shortcoming I shamelessly blame on my husband. He will vouch that, as a single person, I deliberately avoided tasty sauces and seasonings of all kinds. In fact, one of my staple dinner contributions during our first summer of marriage was white rice mixed with a little pack of frozen peas, carrots, and corn. That was it. That was the meal. And though I thoughtfully set out salt and pepper alongside it, I kind of purposefully avoided adding anything that would make veggies from the freezer taste *too good*. As if that were possible.

Today, seventeen years into marriage, I know that the meals I concoct are still mostly tasteless, but if I ask very nicely, my husband will stand over the stove waving powders and potions and—like magic!—a bowl of chili or pot of soup will suddenly taste good.

So now that I actually enjoy them, I find out sixteen years too late that, according to Gregory, the road to hell is paved with sauces and seasonings.

**4. *Quantity*. Exceeding the necessary amount of food.**
Check. Done. Accomplished.

**5. *Eagerness*. Taking food with too much eagerness, even when eating the proper amount, and even if the food is not luxurious.**
Even as I eat the proper amount of nonluxurious frozen mixed vegetables, I could still sin by eating them too "eagerly." And I guarantee that I would. If I'm no longer eating between meals to satisfy my lustful palate, and I'm not sneaking Cheetos onto my plate at lunchtime to gratify my vile sense of taste, and I've eliminated the sauces and seasonings to which I've now grown quite accustomed, and if I haven't been exceeding the necessary amount of food hourly throughout the day, you can darn well bet I'm going to eat *eagerly*.

If there were such a thing as the gluttony police, they would have a field day with me.

## The Gateway Sins

It's not just the gluttony. Let's say that, in addition to gluttony, Sin Monitors were trolling around looking for committers of the other six deadly sins. Though you won't be struck dead if you commit them, they're bad news because they're all the *gateway* sins.

Seven centuries ago, the useful mnemonic SALIGIA, from the first letter (in Latin) of each of the seven deadly sins, reminded penitents of the seven sins. Today, though, these vices that have been taught by the church for centuries have become, for many Americans, sort of more like the seven . . . awesome . . . *goals*.

Were SALIGIA to come back into fashion today, it might be posted as a banner ad on Facebook or printed in a cool font on a black T-shirt. Or maybe it would be on the cover of the most recent release from Lady Gaga.

S is for *superbia* or pride. Desire to be more important or attractive than others.

A is for *avaritia* or greed. Pursue wealth, status, and power.

L is for *luxuria* or lust. Indulge your sexual fantasies.

I is for *individia* or envy. Resent people who have what you want.

G is for *gula* or gluttony. Overconsume all kinds of stuff.

I is for *ira* or wrath. Nurse feelings of anger and hatred.

A is for *acedia* or sloth. Neglect to do what you ought with the gifts and talents you've been given.

You see what I mean when I say that the seven cardinal vices we're instructed to avoid could be an orientation manual for modern American values and practices? I simply confess that I knock off the majority of these on any given day.

## Glad I'm Better Than That Guy

So, Religious folks had called Jesus a glutton. While gluttony is not a high priority on my list of sins with which to condemn others and myself, it has simply opened my eyes to the ways in which I am inclined to overlook *my* sins in a scramble to identify *someone else's* sins. My visual image of "glutton" as that pudgy, shifty-looking guy in Hieronymous Bosch's painting has been exposed as fraud, and I'm left, once again, with the realization that I'm as fraught with sin as the next guy . . . or that guy in the painting.

This is a moment when the classic phrase "when you point a finger at someone else, there are three fingers pointing back at you" really comes home to roost.

# 11

• • • • •

# the nutty logic

If you're with them, you're for them. And if you're *for* them, you can't be *for* us.

I was ten years old, and I had been given an ultimatum.

"If you want to be friends with me, you can't be friends with Sarah," Nellie had announced to me on the way out to recess.

My friend's name wasn't really Nellie, but I want you to imagine the wealthy blonde bully who would have been Laura Ingalls Wilder's hair-pulling, eye-scratching, evil arch-nemesis if Laura hadn't been so well-parented and good-natured.

Fake-Nellie and I had been close friends for two years, and her sudden bossy insistence surprised me. I knew that she and Sarah had had their differences, but there was no reason I needed to be dragged into it. Sarah and I hadn't dipped Nellie's pigtails in an inkwell, nor were we even conspiring to. All we were doing was trading awesome puffy stickers. And though I didn't quite have the ability to articulate why, Nellie's insistence just didn't sit right with me. But painfully good-natured myself, I chose the easy route and simply shied away from Sarah for the rest of the school year.

Though Sarah moved away, and Nellie and I drifted apart in middle school, I continued to dwell on the conflict. The truth was, I felt ashamed for dumping Sarah for no good reason.

Nellie had decided a couple of things for herself and for me. First, Nellie had decided that if I was *with* Sarah, then I was *for* Sarah. And it so happened that this one, which may not have bothered another girl the way it threatened Nellie, was probably true. Guilty. Second, and more troubling, Nellie had also decided that if I was *for* Sarah, then I couldn't be *for* her. This one wasn't true at all. I never once agreed to those weird rules.

I could, in fact, be *for* my friend and, simultaneously, *for* her enemy. For me, the two were not mutually exclusive and, if I'd had my wits about me, I would have said so. In Nellie's mind, though, driven by her insecurity, the two could not be reconciled. So, against my better judgment, I got tangled up by grade-school logic and dropped Sarah like a hot potato.

Unfortunately, the same logic prevails at times in the adult (well . . . adult*ish*) world today. One woman is outraged when her ex is personally invited to the church's spring retreat. A man is irked to see the pastor publically lunching with *him*. Basically, your allegiance to me is threatened if I suspect you're in cahoots with that other one.

This does not bubble up from a healthy place, people.

## Leadership Exercised

Every month or so, something scandalous or titillating will happen in American Christendom that has all of us Christian bloggers riled up for a while. John Piper will tweet adieu to Rob Bell. Mark Driscoll will post a disparaging question on Facebook about gender identity. Don Miller will wax poetic on male/female relationships on his blog.

One of the more recent (as of this writing) cyber uproars was about Starbucks CEO Howard Schultz canceling a recent engagement to speak at Willow Creek's annual Global Leadership Summit. Don't worry, he wasn't suddenly hospitalized for heat exhaustion. He wasn't stranded overseas due to an unforeseeable weather situation. And as far as we know, there had been no pressing family crisis.

Rather, as Willow Pastor Bill Hybels explained on YouTube, protesters had circulated an online petition to boycott Starbucks if Schultz spoke at the summit. The reason cited was that Willow Creek Community Church was "antigay." Hybels explained that the petition had been signed by 717 people.

The petitioners wanted to make it clear to Schultz: "If you're friends with *them*, you can't be friends with *us*."

As I painted this drama for my husband, who wouldn't be caught dead either tweeting or reading a blog, he was more gracious than I. Generously, my devil's-advocate husband was willing to entertain the possibility that these petitioners were practicing some sort of peaceful civil disobedience.

It really felt more like playground bullying to me.

For starters, these petitioners weren't asking Starbucks to legislate fair hiring practices. They weren't asking Starbucks to end discrimination against LGBT people in the workplace. They weren't lobbying the corporation to extend benefits to gay couples. If I'm not mistaken, all of those things actually do seem to fall under the category of civil rights.

Rather, these lobbyists were asking a public figure *not to communicate* with a gathered group of over 150,000 people because of what the petitioners believe—but don't really know for sure—the organization stands for.

"If you're *with* them, you're *for* them. And if you're *for* them, you can't be *for* us. And did we mention? We buy a *lot* of coffee."

## Jesus

If you feel I've sketched an unfair caricature of these irked coffee drinkers, I get that. For what it's worth, I'm clear that the shoe could just have easily been on the right foot as it could on the left foot. If Starbucks started printing a rainbow flag on every cup of coffee served, I'm sure there might be folks gathered for the Leadership Summit who would drop their whipped mocha lattes on the floor, boycott the biz, and encourage their friends to do the same. (I don't think Bill Hybels would do that weird thing, but maybe someone would.)

If you're *for* them, then there's simply no way I can be *for* you.

Scouring the Gospels, I find no evidence that this tragic human logic ruled the mind of Jesus. Rather, Jesus's words and actions bore witness to the fact that Jesus was moved by an entirely different compass.

Because my Father is *for* me, and because my Father is *for* you, I am *for* you. I trust you can recognize how this is a diametrically different proposition. This other way, this Jesus way, is saturated with the logic of love.

## Fired from Macy's

I've mentioned how I'm a sucker for those sidebar links attached to an article I'm reading online. I really am. Today, my choices were:

Macy's Worker Fired for Transgender Discrimination

World Watches and Waits for Euro Rescue

Regardless of the import of the Euro crisis, I don't think I'd read *any* article whose title includes, "Watches and Waits."

Whatever it is we're watching and waiting for—a lunar eclipse, the birth of a lime-green penguin, or the long-awaited release of Willy Wonka's full-meal bubble gum—I don't need to read about the waiting. Instead of wasting my time, just get back to me when you've got some solid intel.

The subhead regarding the Macy's worker pulled me deeper into the unfolding drama: "Natalie Johnson told a transgendered customer to use the men's fitting room."

If . . . theoretically . . . I'd been feeling a little judgie that some bullheaded employee had hassled a colleague or customer whose life was already hard enough, the explanation below ABC's short online video would have stopped me in my combat boot–shaped tracks.[1]

Suddenly, I could easily imagine myself standing in Natalie Johnson's sensible work flats. She'd learned in associate training that men use the men's fitting room and women use the women's fitting room. Trying to be a good employee, I could easily imagine myself thoughtlessly waving my arm toward the men's dressing room. Poor Natalie. Out of work. Not her fault. Well, that stinks!

Then I watched and listened.

The twenty-seven-year-old employee explained that she'd already been eyeing the customer, "I made sure to keep a close eye on him, because he was shopping for women's clothing."

Because, I'm assuming, the reason retail associates keep an extra close eye on certain customers is that they suspect the customer might commit some malicious act on store property, it sounded a little bit as if Ms. Johnson may have collapsed the terms *transvestite*, *transgender*, *thoughtful boyfriend*, or *brother buying birthday present* with *thief*. So she kept a good watch on him.

Macy's policy states that customers may use the dressing room of the gender with whom they associate. In listening to the story, it was unclear whether or not Johnson was aware of this policy when she confronted the customer.

When the customer tried to enter the women's changing room, she prohibited him from doing so. Johnson explains, "I had to just straightforward tell him, 'You're a man.' And of course that really got him steamed up."

Following the incident, when Johnson made it clear to her supervisors that she refused to comply with the policy, she was fired. She then proceeded to file a complaint with the Federal Employment Commission, claiming that her Religious beliefs prevented her from recognizing transgender people.

I had to poke around a little bit to find out what religion she was claiming that prevented her from recognizing transgender people. I had my fingers crossed that it wouldn't be one involving Jesus.

Bad news.

Johnson claims it was her Christian faith that influenced her action. A Christian organization, oddly named Liberty Council, supported Johnson's actions. I think we might be working with different definitions of liberty here.

I certainly agree that Johnson has a right to live her life according to the value system she has embraced. Heartbreaking, though, was her posture of disregard for another individual created in God's image. Tragic, and unchristian, was her refusal to recognize the person standing before her.

Johnson announced, "There are no transgenders in the world."

Really?

Then the sun rotates around the earth. Which is flat. Denying reality—one which is admittedly difficult, messy, and confusing—does not make it any less so. Though Ms. Johnson may not know any transgender folks personally, there are actually a number of people who do experience the world this way. To be transgender is to self-identify one's gender—as a woman, a man, neither, or both—in a way that doesn't match one's assigned sex, or the way they're identified by others. To experience one's self in this way is no more "chosen" than a more normative heterosexuality is *chosen*. While many may find this orientation confusing, and though we may have to work really hard to understand how transgender individuals experience the world, to say that there "are no transgenders" in the world is to build a wall where there might have been a bridge.

Johnson insisted, "A guy can dress up as a woman all he wants, that's still not going to make you a woman."

Denying the experience (again, one that is admittedly difficult, messy, and confusing) of another does not sound anything like the name being invoked to justify dehumanizing another—the name of Jesus.

## Love Is an Orientation

In his award-winning book *Love Is an Orientation*, my friend Andrew Marin shares some of his journey out of denial as he built relationships with folks in the LGBT community. Though his wasn't a confrontational denial, like Johnson's, he sort of freaked out when the first of three friends, in succession, confided in him that they were gay.

Andrew describes his initial visceral response . . .

*Is she serious?!* I tried to pull myself together and look cool, like I had known all along, but I knew I was breathing heavy—I was totally flustered. The horror, pain and dumbfoundedness I felt shook me. She didn't look like a lesbian . . . I knew she had boyfriends . . . I'd even met them! What is going on? I looked her dead in the eyes and panicked. Is there a right response?

I took a shaky breath and promptly said, "OK then, what's to eat?"

The next morning I woke up feeling strange, almost like there had been a death in my family. But I thought, *If I can pretend long enough that she didn't come out to me, I can actually keep my best friend.*[2]

Having also experienced such an emotional blow myself, which feels like getting hit by a speeding train, when a loved one came out to me when I was young, I can relate to Andy's disorientation. Specifically, seemingly outside of his control, his automatic response was denial. She didn't look like a lesbian. She had boyfriends. What's for dinner?

In her 1969 book *On Death and Dying*, Elisabeth Kübler-Ross identifies five recognizable stages of grief people experience when they deal with tragedy. Whether they've been diagnosed with a terminal illness, lose a loved one, or experience another catastrophic loss, these states are typical of their grieving process. They're not linear. One or more might be skipped entirely. A sufferer may return to one previously experienced, or might even get stuck in one. These five wily stages include denial, anger, bargaining, depression, and acceptance.

Though I doubt Andrew would ever name the life-changing encounters he experienced when his friends came out to him as "tragic," he still had to learn to face a new reality that he had not anticipated. His instinctive response was denial.

> If I can pretend long enough that she didn't come out to me,
> I can actually keep my best friend.

When Barbara Walters revealed her ten most fascinating people of 2011, "one" of the people was a couple. Appearing together were *Modern Family* stars Jesse Tyler Ferguson and

Eric Stonestreet, who portray the gay couple Mitch and Cam in the popular ABC comedy. Real-life actors Ferguson and Stonestreet are, respectively, gay and straight. Ferguson spoke graciously about the growth process he and his father have both experienced as they navigate life together as straight-father-with-gay-son. Without a hint of judgment, Ferguson smiles as he remembers visits home when his father would ask, "So do you have a girlfriend?"

Denial.

In consecutive months, three of Andrew's close friends came out to him. In a fog, he would admit that, at first, the experience was very self-focused. It was about him. Why would God give *him* these three friends?

It's what we do. We're not able to be fully present to others.

Andrew describes the conversation that finally happened when he gathered these three friends together. In one fell swoop of nervous energy, he burst out,

> I believe that being gay is a sin. It's a choice. You can change. You're going to hell. You're going to start obsessively drinking and doing drugs. You're going to be promiscuous. You're going to be butch and flamboyant and you're going to get HIV/AIDS or STDs at some point. Now give me something that explains what I feel! Help me understand![3]

I'm delighted to report that their conversation got better after that. It sort of had to, right?

> We talked until the early hours of the morning. Each shared about their lives—what life was like trying to deal with these thoughts and feelings on their own, what it was like to have me as a best friend [snicker], how they weren't sure whether they were right or wrong, weird or normal, sinful or not sinful, whether this was nature or nurture, their fault or God's fault.[4]

111

Andrew's initial blurted response was about him: his beliefs, his opinions, his advice, his theology, his suspicions, and his fears. But after he'd taken a deep breath and gotten his head on straight, he was finally able to listen and look and care about the experiences and thoughts and feelings of his friends. And it's what he's done with his life every day since then.

## But . . .

"But isn't that like approving?"

"Isn't that condoning?"

"If Natalie Johnson had stayed silent, wouldn't that be accepting?"

"If Andrew hadn't blurted out all those weird things, wouldn't that be like affirming?"

That's the sound of the fearful voice many of us hear in our heads. It says, "Don't look. Don't listen. Don't touch. Don't respect." Fueled by our anxieties, it's what keeps us from relationships with those we've identified as Special Sinners. That which keeps us from looking and hearing, from really seeing and listening to an *other*, is our own fear.

So, under the shabby guise of our religiosity, we deny not just the experience of the person in front of us, we deny them.

"There are no transgenders."

"But you had boyfriends!"

"You're no longer welcome here."

One day, though, the light comes on. We realize what we've done. When the rooster crows we realize that by our denial we have ignored, dehumanized, and despised the very ones we were meant to love. And like Peter, at the moment we hear the cock crow, the proper response is to weep bitterly.

# 12

· · · · · ·

# wordless communication

Sometimes Christians like me can be a little tone deaf when we're listening to the Scriptures or liturgies or confessions of the church. As long as someone is saying theologically orthodox words, offering the right magical incantation, we're satisfied. But in every other sector of life, *how* we say what we say matters as much as the words themselves.

A furious older sibling lashes out at an irritating sister, "Baby!"

A lover, taken by the beauty of his beloved, whispers, "Baby."

The message of each is clear.

An abusive partner hisses, "You're a friggin' mess." The words seethe with hatred.

A best bosom buddy laughs, "You're a friggin' mess." The words drip with unconditional affection.

Big difference, right?

In 1994 Newt Gingrich was among those who suggested—quite diplomatically—that the money saved on welfare cuts aimed at minor mothers, and the mothers of children whose paternity was not established, could be used to establish and run orphanages for the children of these now-destitute ones. He cited the 1938 Mickey Rooney film *Boys Town*, about an orphanage for hooligans, as proof that this was not a bad idea at all. His tone was aggressive, trite, and cold.

I contrast Gingrich's position—stance, face, voice, eyes, posture—toward single mothers who receive welfare assistance with a man named Scott I met on a plane from Houston to San Salvador. Though I am typically not a friendly person on airplanes—at all—I did strike up a little dialogue with this guy because he was wearing a Compassion International hat. My first visit to El Salvador had been with Compassion and Scott and I did, in fact, know of a few of the same people there.

Scott and his wife, Sally, I learned, sponsored fourteen children through Compassion around the globe. He would have the opportunity to meet one of them on this trip. He was as excited about this as a child on his way to the circus. Then he described their usual date night.

"Instead of going out on a date, we'll go to a thrift store where single mamas are hanging out," he tells me. "Usually Sally does the interaction with the ladies, because it's a lady thing. So, we'll take 'em shopping . . ."

As he thinks about taking these women shopping for what they need, he gets a little smile on his face—that they're able to get what they need clearly makes him very happy.

". . . and buy 'em groceries."

His eyes glisten, and it's clear that Scott, old enough to be their dad, holds these young women in his heart.

"And sometimes they can't afford what they need at the thrift store, or whatever. If you go in there, God will lead you to 'em." He looks down at the ground and then back up. Clearly emotional, now, he confirms, "It works."

Affection for these precious women in precarious situations exudes from the pores of this motorcycle-riding grizzly bear of a man.

In the Republican Party's 1994 "Contract With America," Gingrich never needs to say that he's not particularly fond of poor, young, single mothers. And Scott never has to come right out and say that he and his wife are head over heels in love with the same women.

In fact, I'm willing to wager a bet. I suspect that Newt could say, "We'll go to a thrift store where single mamas are hanging out. We'll take 'em shopping and buy 'em groceries . . ." and it could still be saturated with vitriol. At the same time, if Scott suggested creating an orphanage for the children of folks who were financially destitute because we'd cut the aid they'd been receiving, I might—against my better judgment—think it was a genius idea.

It's not that my brain doesn't function properly, either. It's that *meaning* is actually communicated through tone.


## An Unlikely Pair

A first-century Samaritan woman was drawing water when another traveler, Jesus, struck up a conversation with her next to an ancient watering hole called Jacob's well.

"Why on earth are you talking to me?" she responds.

In relation to Jesus, this Samaritan woman was the wrong gender. She was the wrong race. She was the wrong religion. She was unholy. With absolutely no reason at all to interact with a sojourning Jewish man—ever—on no morning did she wake up and think, *Maybe I'll chat it up with a Jewish man at the well today.* It just didn't happen.

Unlike most Jewish travelers, who would have looped safely around the outer edge of town, Jesus and his buddies traveled right through the middle of Samaria. When you think of Samaria, you should think of whatever neighborhood it is in your city that you, and others of your ilk, avoid at all costs. The people were dirty and the route was dangerous. So, not surprisingly, this was the route that Jesus chose to travel.

His friends had all gone to the local grocery store to get lunch, and Jesus, tired from the journey, had hung back to chill and regroup at Jacob's well. Traveling light, thirsty Jesus hadn't even brought a water bottle. So when a local woman came to fetch water, Jesus asked her for a drink.

When this Jewish man opened his mouth, she might rightfully have expected some sort of slur or insult. So when he was kind, I think she probably did that thing where—because it's so very unlikely that a person is speaking to *you*—you turn your head to see if someone is standing right behind you. But there wasn't anyone there. He was speaking to *her*. He'd relinquished the power of at *least* his gender, making himself vulnerable by asking her for a drink of water.

As their conversation continues, the barriers to relationship are lowered even further when Jesus reveals that he's in possession of some kind of super-water by which this woman will never be thirsty again. When she says she'd like to try some, he instructs her to go get her husband.

"I have no husband," she replies (see John 4:17).

Now this is where it gets really good.

### Response

Jesus responds to her. John, the writer of the Gospel in which this story is found, doesn't tell us if Jesus used a harsh judgmental tone like some folks do when talking to or about a woman of ill repute. John doesn't indicate if Jesus used a sarcastic, jovial tone, like a goofy teenage boy trying to be clever

116

when cracking a joke about her not having *one* husband. John doesn't indicate if Jesus spoke in a purposefully nondescript tone, like flight attendants do when they're describing what to do in the event of a horrible emergency, so they don't alarm anyone. He doesn't let on if Jesus is speaking as if he's caught someone with her hand in the cookie jar: "Aha! I finally caught you! Your secret is out! You're not fooling me, young lady."

No, instead, all we get are the words themselves:

> You are right when you say you have no husband. The fact is, you have had five husbands, and the man you now have is not your husband. What you have just said is quite true. (John 4:17–18)

When *you* listen to these words, how do they sound in your ear?

The voice I hear is one I heard, very briefly, almost twenty years ago.

## Cooper Hospital

During grad school I was volunteering at Cooper Hospital in Camden, New Jersey, as a candy striper. A candy striper is sort of like an earthbound flight attendant. She—or he?—is the person who, wearing a red and white dress and resembling a human candy cane, passes out magazines, water, and extra pillows to patients. The candy stripers of the 1950s wore the dresses, anyway. I just wore regular clothes. Once I'd done my rounds, and had offered cool water to patients in the twelve little rooms on the unit to which I'd been assigned, I'd return to a bench in the hallway to wait for someone to get thirsty again.

As I sat there one Sunday afternoon, memorizing Greek vocabulary flash cards, one of the patient aids, a large African

American woman, sat down and struck up a conversation with me. I was, initially, a little surprised that she even noticed nerdy little me. Not only that, but for a few minutes she showed a real interest in me. Though I don't remember much of our conversation at all now, I will never forget what she *called* me.

She called me "baby."

It wasn't *baby* in the nasty second-grade playground way, or in a sleazy pickup line way, or even the newborn "goochy goochy goo" way. She called me baby in the warm, affectionate, gracious, tender way in which some wise and older women seem to specialize. Though the exchange was brief, in those wonderful moments what her face, body, and voice all communicated to me were, "You're alright, baby. You're gonna make it." As she wandered off to help someone else, someone who'd actually come to the hospital *knowing* they were going to be on the receiving end of help, I may have even heard audible strains of *The Five Stairsteps* singing, "Ooh child, things are gonna get easier. Ooh child, things will get brighter."

In a sterile institutional hallway, from a woman whose name I did not know, I received the gift of gracious presence and acceptance for which human beings most long. To this day I still feel all melty when big black women call me *baby*.

## The Lady

Though I can't physically *hear* the tone of Jesus's voice the way I *heard* the peaceful assurance in the hospital aid's voice, I can hazard a guess based on the Samaritan woman's response to his words.

By all outward indicators, this conversation should have gone badly. Very badly. For starters, this stranger, Jesus, pinpoints this woman's sin: she's had five husbands and now she's shacking up with some new guy. In my own life, very few people get away with this sort of truth-telling. And even then—my husband will be quick to confirm this—they escape with their lives only by the hair of their chinny chin chins. That a stranger divinely intuits one's sin makes it no more palatable than when it comes from a loved one. That the conversation then turns to the spiritual differences between Jews and Samaritans only makes it seem all the more destined for ruin.

What I wouldn't give to have been a fly-on-the-well so that I could physically *hear* these very words spoken by Jesus. Given the bitter animosity between Jews and Samaritans, the woman would have expected them to be laced with judgment. And even though there was no secret voice-recorder chip built into a 007 pocket pen clipped to Jesus's lapel, I know that his words weren't sticky with judgment, for several reasons.

For starters, the woman *physically* stuck around. She didn't huff off the way some people might when a stranger gets all up in their business. Secondly, the woman continues to converse with him, even identifying him as a prophet. Thirdly, she trusts him enough to bend the conversation in a spiritual direction. Lastly, when his disciples return, surprised to find him talking to a woman, she races back to town to tell folks that she may have just found the Messiah.

That Jesus's words did not shut her down, but rather opened her up, says *everything* about the tone in which they were spoken. They hint at a gracious expression on Jesus's face. They suggest a welcoming posture. They reveal a woman who did not experience being known and *judged*, but known and *loved*. Those two things are so different.

That an identified Sinner runs to tell the people in her town to come and see a man who'd told her everything she'd ever done gives a pretty strong indication which type of encounter she'd had with Jesus.

# 13
• • • • •

# baby killers and the surprise of identifying with monstrous sinners

Monsters.

That is what one neighbor called two teens who lived in a nearby New Jersey town in 1996.

My neighbor Penny cared for elderly folks at a local long-term care facility. She was quick to see what was good and valuable and precious in every individual, even those whom society would have cruelly deemed worthless. I think that this is one of the reasons I was surprised by her sharp unyielding judgment of Amy and Brian.

## Desperate Measures

Before their story was ever made into a *Law and Order* episode, Amy Grossberg and Brian Peterson were accused of killing their newborn child at a Comfort Inn motel in Newark, Delaware.

Both teens had been raised in an affluent New York suburb, and had dated as high school students. Amy had conceived during her final semester as a high school senior. Effectively hiding her pregnancy from her parents over the summer months, she enrolled as a freshman at the University of Delaware in the fall of 1996.

It's not at all clear to me what the couple was thinking during this period of time. This wasn't a case for one of TLC's riveting *I Didn't Know I Was Pregnant* episodes. Amy knew she was pregnant. And yet while most women who are pregnant make some sort of plan—to abort or deliver, to raise a child or relinquish her for adoption—these two smart, affluent, educated college freshman had no clear plan. They were, it seems, in denial.

When Amy's water broke on November 12, she phoned Brian, who attended college in Gettysburg, Pennsylvania, three hours away. "Water breaking" means that, for safety's sake, women must deliver within twenty-four hours. After driving to Delaware and picking her up, Brian checked them into the Comfort Inn in Newark, where Amy gave birth.

A cleaning woman later found bloody sheets in the hotel dumpster. After authorities were summoned, police dogs discovered the infant's dead body, also in the dumpster. When Amy began suffering seizures as a result of not passing the baby's placenta, she was taken to a hospital. There authorities put the pieces together and were able to identify her as the dead child's mother.

The couple claimed the child had been stillborn, but an autopsy concluded the baby had been born alive and had died as a result of head fractures and shaken baby syndrome. However, experts in the 1997 trial expressed different opinions about whether or not the baby was alive or dead upon birth. Though critics have been forced to admit that the only two people on earth who will ever know for sure are Peterson and Grossberg, I am willing to entertain the possibility that even these two might not know for sure.

## Monstrous Otherness

When Penny stopped to chat on the sidewalk, she had definitively pronounced that the teens were monsters.

If you've seen any of the *Shrek* movies, or *Beauty and the Beast*, or *Edward Scissorhands*, or *How to Train Your Dragon*, you know that *monster* is the epitomy of otherness. We project all that we despise within us onto the monster. Whether or not the other is an actual threat becomes irrelevant. Because we do not *know* monster, it comes to symbolize all that is evil. Banishing, excluding, isolating, or killing the monster, we decide as an angry mob, will keep us safe from its evils.

Why did I not see them as monsters, when Penny clearly did? I suspect that I simply could not be sure that a similarly hideous form of self-protecting malevolence could never take root in my own heart.

## Judge or Judged?

As we engage with the biblical narrative, we might also find ourselves siding against a Sinner. Like my friend Penny, we might—if we're able to be very honest with ourselves—feel very strongly that a Sinner ought to get whatever nasty fate they deserve. For instance, in the case of the unfortunate woman caught in adultery, the deepest impulse of some of our hearts, though we're savvy enough not to admit it in good Christian company, is that we're really sort of glad she got caught. And maybe we're a little disappointed there wasn't a stoning. Others of us—the ones who might just as easily be dragged before some moral tribunal—can only breathe a deep sigh of both relief and gratitude at her unexpected good fortune. We're the ones who fall down on our faces thanking Jesus for his mercy because we know ourselves well enough to realize that, on another day, we could be standing right where her bare feet were planted.

If it's not clear to you on just which side of the judgment scale you land, and since it is insanely easy to fool ourselves, I have for you yet another fun party trick. Remember when Jesus meets Zacchaeus and goes to his house, and Zacchaeus promises to pay back all he's stolen? You remember that story?

What is *good news* in that story?

If you find yourself *most satisfied* that Zacchaeus, the underdog, the wretched Sinner, comes out on top, then it's very likely you've identified with the Judged.

If you are secretly more pleased that, as a result of his encounter with Jesus, Zacchaeus changes his behavior, you have most likely identified with the Judge.

If you think the good news is that Sinners are welcomed by Jesus, then you've identified with the Judged.

If you think it's good news that Sinners finally get their act together and start acting right, then you've identified with the Judge.

Ironically, I'm not suggesting any of this to judge you. I'm just saying that if the good news really is that Sinners are welcomed by Jesus, and you're not really able to identify with Sinners, then the news might not be so good for you.

## Tiger

Tiger Woods's first television spot for Nike, in 1997, featured a rainbow of young children—caddying, toting bulky bags of golf clubs, practicing their swings—repeating the words, "I am Tiger Woods." The children are of all ages, rich and poor, Asian, European, African, and mixed-race. The inspirational soundtrack, and children of color tromping around golf courses and country clubs to which their grandparents could never have gained admission, almost brings a tear to the eye. The ad, of course, was about hope and promise and possibility. In 1997 Tiger Woods had become a role model to which *all* children could aspire.

When Tiger Woods's infidelity hit the national news in 2009, the commercial suddenly had a different ring than it had twelve years earlier.

We are quick to identify with winners, and quicker still to dissociate from losers, so Tiger Woods—the *other* who had become *us*, and whom we aspired to become—became *other* once again. Suddenly no one was saying, "I am Tiger Woods."

## Off the Hook

I recently realized that I play this same game when I read Scripture. Though I'm quick to identify with Jesus, and pattern my life after his, I would much prefer to distance myself from some of the mangy mutts with whom he involved himself.

More often than not, when I have really quieted myself and listened hard, I hear my inner-Margot insisting, time and time again, "I'm not *that* guy."

For instance, I'm not the lost sheep because . . . obviously . . . that misfit is probably a Hindu or a Buddhist. If I were "lost," I wouldn't be in the third pew of church every week.

I'm not the priest who, going down the road where some poor bloke had just been mugged and beaten, does that thing where you walk on the other side of the street so it seems like you don't notice the bloody person lying by the road, even though you totally do. I give Band-Aids to kids who get scraped while playing at my house *all the time.* So, clearly, I'm not that guy!

I'm not the rich young ruler for . . . well . . . I guess just for those three descriptors. I'm not the prodigal son because I'm not one of those who has turned to wild sex and drugs for comfort. Just Ben & Jerry's.

I'm not. I'm not. I'm not.

This isn't to say that I don't identify with *anyone* in these stories. Because I do. I very much relate to the Good Samaritan, probably because of all the Band-Aids I've dispensed over the years. I AM that person. And as a mom, I really relate to the shepherd with well-developed biceps and triceps from carrying home so many lost sheep. I AM that person. And since I'm a bona fide ministry professional, I also have a lot of answers to share with questioning folks such as the rich young ruler. I AM that person. And again, with the parenting, I'm a little like the dad who welcomes home his wayward child. I AM that person.

When I finally pause to notice how I do relate to Scripture, it really proves quite remarkable how consistently I am able to identify myself as the Savior figure who redeems the lost.

## Experiment

So, just as an experiment, I started plowing through the Gospels with an "I am Tiger Woods" attitude. I was curious to see what would happen if I played that imaginary game. So I tried it.

I am the aloof priest.
I am the rich young ruler.
I am the lost sheep.

I am the prodigal son.

I am. I am. I am. I am.

What happened really surprised me.

Pretending to be a person in need of grace felt not foreign, but instead *authentic*. Though this should not really have been news, I confess that it was. I had begun the Religious exercise under the illusion that, to identify with Sinners, to stand in the shoes of the misguided, recalcitrant, and lost, I would need to slip on the costume of the sinful. I thought I'd need to use my most creative mind to construct a world in which I was in desperate need of saving.

Something else, though, transpired instead.

What I found as I slipped into the worn, beaten shoes of the *other* was not the expected weight of the disguise I imagined donning. Rather than feeling heavier under the weight of a costume, I experienced the kind of lightness that comes from removing a wet, heavy, wool jacket.

Becoming the other, embracing neediness, identifying as Sinner felt so much lighter and freer and *more real* than the damp, mildewed weight of my goodness façade.

## Courthouse Supporters

In 2005 singer Michael Jackson was tried for child molestation. For weeks, throngs of supporters gathered outside the courthouse to show their support for the man being accused by the family of a thirteen-year-old boy. Since everyone waving a sign or wearing a single imitation silver-studded glove couldn't possibly have known him personally, I have to assume that many were simply . . . enthusiastic fans.

Like a predominant number of white Americans, I was baffled that anyone—no matter how intimately they may have known the defendant—could offer their unequivocal support for someone accused of such crimes. I simply couldn't fathom how anyone who wasn't physically in the room at the moment of the alleged incident could possibly know what had happened between Jackson and his accuser. I didn't know if he *was* guilty, but I certainly couldn't say for sure that he was not.

Witnessing the unflagging confidence of these supporters, many of whom were black, was when I knew that something very unwieldy happens in the human heart and mind when we identify, or don't identify, with an *other*.

Frankly, I was baffled by the confidence of these rabid supporters. (Though I don't want to attribute this to my whiteness, I'm willing to consider the possibility.) Now, had some sleazy paparazzi planted a score of secret video cameras throughout Jackson's Neverland ranch, recording his every move, I might have had a wee bit more sympathy for his sympathizers. Had one of those cameras caught a thirteen-year-old boy planting evidence or bragging about his genius plan to take the innocent artist to the cleaners, I'd be even less concerned about all the support.

I just know that very attractive, very talented, very charming people have been shown to do some very bad things.

I was, and remain, entirely convinced that it's just not possible for the average television news–watching citizen to ever *really* know, in cases like these. As a matter of fact, I'm enough of a realist to believe that a defendant's closest friends and family members wouldn't even know, for sure, whether or not their loved one was capable of such malevolence. In the most traumatic cases, especially those involving children, the actual victim might not even retain a clear memory of the incident. And I understand the same goes for the perpetrators.

Because our minds play funny tricks, my firm conviction remains that you can never *really* know for sure what transpires on dark sidewalks or behind closed doors.

## Passionate

This conviction is what made my own behavior on the morning of March 26, 2006, unlikely, embarrassing, and confusing.

That was the morning I pulled my seven-year-old daughter out of Sunday school in Durham, North Carolina, in order to march her into a pulsing mob of angry strangers at the site of an alleged assault. Specifically, we lent our presence to a protest in front of the house rented by some Duke lacrosse players suspected of sexual assault. Upon arrival I placed a canvas I had painted near the house. Showing angry faces, dashed with serious black and angry red, it announced—as if there was any question about the fact—"Durham Residents Are Outraged!"

Though many of the revelers had thought to bring their favorite pots and pans for noisemaking, I'd left mine at home. So I was left to grab the nearest beer cans littering the lawn. Their disappointingly tiny clinking sound was lost in the cacophony of ladles and frying pans.

The local debacle caused by members of Duke's men's lacrosse team being accused of assaulting an exotic dancer had just hit the news and was about to make national headlines. That the alleged victim was an African American woman and the accused were white men only made the story more salacious.

Though keen readers already know how this one ended, at the time, I did not.

Because I do not like to see myself as a snap-judger, and because a wise friend on the Duke women's lacrosse team had insisted the boys were innocent, I've had to replay this one over and over in my mind. And then over again. How on earth did I become the person who marched around being outraged at someone else's alleged sin while inadvertently spraying beer on her child on a morning when that child would normally be in Sunday school?

## Piecing the Pieces

If there's any way of blaming it on the media, without painting myself as one of these fools who's duped by the media, that's exactly how I'd like to spin it.

The previous day the local news had reported the words of Durham police officer David Addison: "We will be relentless in finding out who committed this crime."

From this, I naturally deduced that a crime had been committed.

When, in an article on the case, the local paper posted a disclaimer that it was their policy not to identify victims of sex crimes, I assumed that the accuser whom they'd interviewed must be a victim of said sex crime.

So in my mind, there was a crime, there was at least one perpetrator, and there was a victim.

Though I had no way of knowing *exactly* what had happened in that house, I had read what seemed to be a reasonable account of facts. It struck me as viable. After all, as the two women who'd been hired to dance at the house got into a car to leave, a neighbor had heard one man yell out a racial slur.

The witness of this random neighbor, someone without a dog in the fight, confirmed in my mind that—if not sexual

130

assault—*something* awful had happened behind closed doors. So although I did not know for certain what it was, I was convinced that a wrong had been committed. A wrong worthy of my outrage.

Soon after, now-infamous and disbarred District Attorney Richard Nifong issued this statement: "The circumstances of the rape indicated a deep racial motivation for some of the things that were done. It makes a crime that is by its nature one of the most offensive and invasive, even more so."

Reference to "the rape," from a trusted public servant no less, confirmed my suspicion that a crime worthy of outrage, with a victim and a perpetrator, had been committed.

That I had not been able to identify the crime correctly, nor even which parties were victims and which were perpetrators, would of course come out in the end. The accuser's story, it turned out, had been the sad ruse of a broken and hurting woman. The painful unraveling of both her story and the lives of all those involved on various levels would gradually expose my shame.

## Ancient Sting Op

There's a story in the Old Testament about a sting operation that I have always loved. Though I'll summarize it here, I recommend reading the whole thing. If you don't own a Bible, this story alone is worth the price of the book. The setup is in 2 Samuel 11. The sting comes in chapter 12.

After impregnating Bathsheba, the wife of another man, King David—on whom the Lord was clearly quite keen—tried to cover his tracks. He went to all the trouble of bringing her husband, Uriah, back from battle to sleep with her. In solidarity with his fellow soldiers, Uriah refused to enjoy the pleasures of home while his army was still at war. The next night, frustrated by the man's untiring honor, David got him all liquored up before sending him home. But after leaving David's palace, Uriah returned to sleep on the ground with his buddies, rather than David's intended destination of Bathsheba's bed.

His wily scheme thwarted, David wrote a sealed letter to Uriah's commanding officer, which was delivered by Uriah himself. The letter instructed the commander to put Uriah at the front of the battle and then retreat, leaving him hanging. As you might imagine, it wasn't long before Bathsheba received word of her husband's untimely demise.

Yikes. Sinners! There's absolutely nothing worse than a righteous Sinner. What are you going to do with them, right?

Some of us who want to let Sinners know how they've really screwed up like to wave and shout and bang on things. Others of us like to legislate. Some choose the route of vigilante justice. At the direction of the Almighty, though, the prophet Nathan told David a little story.

> There were two men in a certain town, one rich and the other poor. The rich man had a very large number of sheep and cattle, but the poor man had nothing except one little ewe lamb he had bought. He raised it, and it grew up with him and his children. It shared his food, drank from his cup and even slept in his arms. It was like a daughter to him.
>
> Now a traveler came to the rich man, but the rich man refrained from taking one of his own sheep or cattle to prepare a meal for the traveler who had come to him. Instead, he took the ewe lamb that belonged to the poor man and prepared it for the one who had come to him.
>
> David burned with anger against the man and said to Nathan, "As surely as the LORD lives, the man who did this must die! He must pay for that lamb four times over, because he did such a thing and had no pity." (2 Sam. 12:1–6)

In my mind's eye, I can almost see David banging together ancient pottery on the rich man's lawn.

Then Nathan said to David, "You are the man!" (v. 7).

And today, Nathan says to me, "You are the woman!" And I am. I really am.

# 14

. . . . .

# clarifying my job description

Upon seeing him attending a rally in support of President Clinton after Clinton's sex scandal had been exposed, a reporter asked mega-preacher Billy Graham, "Why are you here supporting this man after everything he's done to this country?"

I'm thinking it might have been a Christian reporter.

Humbly, without an ounce of the vitriol I'd try to slather on if I'd had the chance to deliver such a zinger, Graham simply confessed, "It is the Holy Spirit's job to convict, God's job to judge, and my job to love."[1]

Which, to the righteous reporter, or any other listener, might have seemed like taking the *easy* way out.

## The Big Plan

About a year and a half ago, when I started noticing how a lot of Christians were aggressively engaging with those they'd identified as Special Sinners—with angry picketing and vicious signs and sandwich-board sound bites—I began to wonder if this was really the Big Plan. When I looked at two snapshots, one of the loud curbside picketers and one of Jesus as he's sketched in the Gospels, there just seemed to be no resemblance between the two whatsoever.

Certain that Jesus had some different plan for twenty-first-century Christians, and that we'd just not stumbled upon it yet, I asked two friends if they'd help me think this through.

I trusted these two, a married couple, implicitly and entirely on all matters related to grace. They had street cred, in my book, because they were actually kicked off the staff of a worldwide gospel-sharing parachurch organization for landing a little too heavy on the side of grace. When they had the opportunity to toe the party line and say, "You're right, God's not as gracious as we once thought," instead they stuck with God's grace and goodness. So I suspected that they'd be able to help me sort out the incongruities between what I was reading in Scripture and how a lot of Christians in the media spotlight were behaving. I emailed them and we decided on a date to sit down together.

After I had briefly summarized my concern about the way the church treats "Special Sinners," you can imagine my disappointment when both husband and wife empathetically commiserated with me. "Yeah, that's so true, isn't it? Wacky!" In the same sea-wandering boat as me, they were useless! Except, of course, I did realize I was not alone in my bafflement and confusion and desire to find a way to live that more closely resembled Jesus.

But as we continued to wrestle, my friend shared a Scripture verse that I never really understood or cared about before: "God's kindness is intended to lead you to repentance" (Rom. 2:4).

Sounding a wee bit too much like that radical, Billy Graham, this possibility immediately seemed too good to be true.

## A Liberating Possibility

Let me just say that even more intriguing than what that verse says is *where* it's said. Paul's announcement, in Romans 2, is adjacent to Romans 1.

If that means nothing to you, then God bless you. Romans 1 is one of a few biblical passages that have been used as battering rams to clobber the LGBT community. It's always a favorite of folks who name homosexuality as a sin. There are plenty of other special sins mentioned there too in Paul's long list of those who don't glorify God or thank him. These include, but are not limited to, those "filled with every kind of wickedness, evil, greed and depravity. They are full of envy, murder, strife, deceit and malice. They are gossips, slanderers, God-haters, insolent, arrogant and boastful; they invent ways of doing evil; they disobey their parents; they have no understanding, no fidelity, no love, no mercy" (vv. 29–31).

Well, this sin list winds down at the end of chapter 1, which I'm really happy about because I feel a little uncomfortable around wrathful God. So the large numeral "2" sort of feels, to a reader, like a protective barrier from the wrathfulness of chapter 1. I understood it to mean that we'd switched subjects and were on to something completely new. That's often what the big numerals mean. As I begin to read, however, I quickly realize that—in the context of a larger argument that can't be neatly parsed simply because there's a large "2" on the page—Paul pivots the sin microscope away from the *other* and toward insiders like me who had, all the while, been busy checking for dirt beneath our fingernails during the sin list about other people, only half-listening.

You, therefore, have no excuse, you who pass judgment on someone else, for at whatever point you judge another, you are condemning yourself, because you who pass judgment do the same things. (2:1)

Umm . . . excuse me? Just who does Paul think he is? Does this guy even *know* me?

A closer inspection of the longer sin list suggests that he might.

Though I wish it were otherwise, no one can look at my credit card statement and claim I don't worship and serve created things. Too often, I do. A mood ring that gauges my rising envy when I see how many comments Rachel Held Evans's blog has garnered in two short hours locates me on the sin list. Anyone tapping phone conversations between my husband and I knows that each sentence I begin with, "Now, this is just between you and me, okay?" is probably gossip, with a dash of slander thrown in for bad measure. And boastfulness? Any professional bio I've penned is *as purposefully boastful* as I can make it. And when I'm trying to hide the wrappers of Little Debbie oatmeal cream pies that I've sneak-eaten and am looking for novel hiding places from my children, I am creating new clever ways to do evil every time. And though it's always a little surprising to me, I suspect no one else is surprised one bit that I'm in the sin doghouse with the murderers.

Paul is suggesting that the point at which I judge others is the precise point at which I bring judgment on myself. When *God* judges, he says, it's based on truth, but when I do it, it's about something else. In judging another, Paul suggests that I am showing "contempt for the riches of his kindness, forbearance and patience" (Rom. 2:4).

That we've shifted so quickly from Angry God to Kind God—the one with kindness, forbearance, and patience—feels a little like whiplash to me.

Paul asks, "Don't you get it, Margot? Do you not understand how this thing works? Or do you show contempt for the riches of God's kindness, forbearance, and patience, not realizing that his kindness is meant to lead you to repentance?"

Wait . . . wait . . . what?

If Paul can be believed—and it's really God's kindness, forbearance, and patience that lead to life-change—then we have simply *got* to change the way we're engaging with Sinners.

This is a real game-changer, people.


## Testimony

My friend Andrew Marin, who builds relationships with the gay community in Chicago, reports that the work of convicting and judging really does belong to God.

Before I provide the data, though, I want to put it in a larger context.

Some Christians who experience feelings of same-sex attraction and are deeply connected to God have heard God's voice blessing their sexual identity. As I report this, I realize that some will find "Gay Christian" to be an oxymoron. You may find it hard to imagine a gay person is listening to the voice of the exact same God you're dialing up each week. I understand. Please be patient. You'll be glad you did.

Though this report, taken from Andrew's fieldwork, may sound entirely offensive to some, others are saying, "Yup, that sounds like the voice of Jesus's dad to me. That is exactly the way that deity operates."

Other Christians who experience feelings of same-sex attraction and are deeply connected to God have heard God's voice letting them know they're *not* actually gay. As I report this, I realize that some will find this to be very pedantic and demeaning. You may find it hard to believe that this person wasn't just a confused mostly heterosexual from the get-go. I understand. Please be patient. You'll be glad you did.

To you, the dubious and the convinced, I share a story that Andrew tells in *Love Is an Orientation*. He'd been hosting a Bible study that was really flourishing. Gay men and women invited their friends and it got bigger and bigger. Curious, one day Andrew asked them, "Why do you come, and why do you invite others to come?"

Then he listened.

Andrew shares, "Those GLBT people in the group related that the Bible study was a breath of fresh air because I didn't focus on their sexuality at all; instead, I unapologetically focused on how to have a better, more intimate relationship with God apart from any GLBT issues."[2] Andrew quickly admits that this apparent strategy had not been part of an intelligent master plan, but rather because he was too scared to say anything about sexuality. Funny, right? The Lord works in mysterious ways.

A few weeks later a number of folks each got Andrew alone and said, "God is telling me that I'm not gay, and I need your help." Andrew, who'd never talked about "change," was baffled. Where had that come from?

The answer?

"You didn't tell me anything. God did."[3] (I know that's very satisfying for some of you who really wanted the story to end that way. Thank you for your patience.)

The truth is, it could have just as easily gone the other way. And, of course, it did—and still does. Connecting independently to God, others heard God say something different.

I'm not saying I understand it, and I'd be suspicious of anyone who claimed they did. I'm saying that when Andrew— humbly, fearfully, awkwardly, unskillfully—let folks know about who God was, made a space for them to study Scripture, and encouraged them to connect with God personally, he effectively stepped out of the way for God to work and speak.

So often I hear echoes of my friend Jeff's voice, asking earnestly, "Do we trust God *enough* to believe that it's his kindness that leads to repentance?"

Billy Graham did.

# 15

•••••

## Jesus in vegas

Linda, a relative of mine, lives in New York City and runs with women in a pretty upscale crowd—though *technically*, I don't believe that any of these women ever *have* to run anyplace. Though each one has excelled in her field—whether in sales or real estate or business or banking—no woman is rushing to punch a time card or racing to catch an uptown bus after a punishing boss has demanded overtime. This is not to say that they haven't put in a respectable number of treadmill miles. Sleek, spray-tanned calves insist they do. Before an upcoming power meeting, they'll run to a chic boutique. When brown roots begin to dirty platinum locks, they run to the salon. When some body part begins to droop, they run to their cosmetic surgeon. *That's* how Linda's crowd runs.

Though I do not know the particular women with whom Linda lunches, their ilk makes me uncomfortable enough to use the word *ilk*. Not only have they graduated from the right colleges and grad schools, they're alumni of the right *elementary* schools. Today their six-year-olds attend the same ones. These women live in the right neighborhoods, drive the right cars, and hire the right help. The dog walkers who scoop their canines' poop are studying veterinary medicine, the nannies who microwave their kids' alphabet soup have graduate degrees in education, and the interior designers whose staff members shop for the room-themed knickknacks on these women's shelves have their own hit television shows on TLC.

Clearly, these females intimidate me. I think that perhaps I feel uncomfortable around this type because the energy I spend worrying that they're judging *me* saps my ability to be judging *them* at the same time. It's really very exhausting.

Linda is a much better person than I am. She really loves these women and wouldn't be caught dead even thinking the word *ilk*. Unlike so many Manhattan social climbers who would gladly give up their coveted parking spaces just to be near them, Linda is with them and loving them as Jesus does. In fact, from what I know of Linda, after she's dropped her kids off at school each morning she probably mutes the sound system in her custom SUV so she can just prayerfully noodle on new ways to love these women.

Though a lot of her values are decidedly different from the ones held by these Women of the Ilk, thankfully Linda is attractive enough, bright enough, charming enough, and successful enough that they let her hang around.

I won't lie. This whole situation has done a number on me. While, as a general rule, I usually cannot whip up an ethical justification for obscene preschool tuition or pricey gym memberships or unnecessary cosmetic surgery, Linda's purposeful care for these women just makes me want to send her a cute little gift card to get a spray tan. Of course I am certainly willing to admit that, spinning from the novelty of it all, I may not be thinking clearly.

Linda tells me that each spring the attractive and successful husbands of these attractive and successful wives dig their cleats and sun visors out of storage and pack up their clubs and monogrammed golf towels to traipse across the country for a weekend of sport. This is what they tell the six-year-olds, anyway. Under the respectable guise of the "golf weekend," though, what they actually *do* when they arrive in Vegas is enjoy the annual porn convention. Though I can't say for sure what else happens there, I've seen the television commercials and I know it can't be good.

This—the social climbing and the desert pornography—apparently is *the life.*

## The Pickle

I'd rattled off this much of the story to my sweaty friend Jamie as we enjoyed our weekly power walk near my home in North Carolina. Since the most prestigious circle in which either Jamie or I currently find ourselves is our kids' elementary school knitting circle, such a racy, upscale social scene was pretty new for both of us.

A wide-eyed Jamie looked a little bit shocked when I told her that Linda was deliberately weighing how deeply she should become involved in these women's social lives. A person of faith who is typically not at all prone to use Religious clichés, Jamie wondered aloud, "What would Jesus do?" It was as good a moment as any to use a cliché. If Jesus had some of these friends—and here I'm assuming he was clever and entertaining enough for them to overlook the whole "blue collar" situation and let him hang around—what would *he* do if they invited him to join them in Sin City?

Sometimes, in sticky ethical situations, it helps to know what Jesus would do. When we've got to decide whether or not to carve a small wooden deity we could worship instead of Jesus's dad, it's nice to know how Jesus would handle the situation. It even comes in handy if we're trying to decide whether or not to covet our neighbor's wife.

Whether or not to *tag along* while someone else is coveting someone else's wife, however, is a whole other thing. On a hunch, I spit out, "Jesus would go to Vegas." Though I hadn't really thought it through, I wanted Jamie to bat it around with me a bit.

That was when Jamie's eyes bugged right out of her sweaty head.

"You're saying," she confirmed, slowly and purposefully, "that you think Jesus would go to Vegas with those guys?"

Sort of pleased I'd rattled her cage, I agreed, "Yup." I felt pretty confident that if he'd descended into hell, he could probably handle himself in the Nevada desert.

When her head spun around 360 degrees, like one of those creepy antique dolls from a horror movie, I realized that maybe I was moving too fast. But because Jamie respected me, I think she really wanted to work with me on it. Trying desperately to reconcile the incoherence of what I'd just proposed, she ventured, "So, he'd *fly* there with them, but he wouldn't go to the convention . . ."

I think she felt okay about Jesus sharing a first-class cabin with these clowns, but I gleaned from her tone that it was really important to her that he wouldn't go to the convention.

I ventured, "I think he'd *love* them." That Sunday school answer is never wrong.

"But what would he *do*?" she demanded. She wanted to know, once they'd caught a shuttle to their hotel and unpacked their bags, exactly how he'd kill time while the guys were enjoying the merchandise, both manufactured and human, at the convention.

A snapshot came to mind of Jesus chilling in his hotel room, clicking through cable channels. His dirty sandaled feet were on the bed since everyone knows those hotel bedspreads are already crawling with germs anyway. Then, opting for something much more spiritual than HGTV, I imagined him kneeling beside that germy bed to pray, careful not to let his jet-lagged face touch it, while making a mental note to scrub his hands and forearms when he was done. Sometimes it's funny how the Jesus in my mind can look so much like me. I imagined a squinty-eyed Savior, knees on the disgusting carpet, praying reverently for his friends in the convention center who'd been led into temptation, begging his Father with every fiber of his being to deliver them from the evil they'd chosen. Maybe that's what he'd do.

Or maybe Jesus would grab the key card to his room and, chiding himself for not wearing a robe-dress with pockets, head down toward the convention. I imagined him somberly walking a reverent perimeter around the property, praying for the walls to fall down in judgment on the whole debacle.

While my musings might have been what *I* would have done in Vegas, if I was honest, they just didn't seem much like the guy who was scorned for partying with Sinners. That there are two strikingly different definitions of *Sinner* floating around my Christian circle always muddies the waters when trying to see these situations clearly.

## Friend of Sinners

Although I am very fond of saying things like "one sin is not worse than another," "all sin separates us from God," and "sin is sin," I've begun to wonder recently whether or not I really mean it. I'm starting to notice that, even as I bellow to the rafters that grace "saved a wretch like me," I don't actually believe that I'm *quite* as wretched as the guy three rows back who got busted by the cops for domestic violence. So while, if cornered, I'll happily admit that I'm a Sinner, all I *really* mean by that is I'm just the same as, and no worse than, everybody else in the room. That's what I mean when I say that *I* am a Sinner.

When I say that someone *else* is a Sinner—or think it privately, since it's not socially appropriate to say a lot of the things I think—I secretly believe that guy behind me is of the breed of Sinner that is, in fact, a little bit worse than the rest of us who haven't been *caught* being violent toward family members. Über-privately, I suspect that the single young woman who accidentally gets pregnant is a teensy weensy bit more sinful than all the rest of us who, by luck or good fortune or nobody asking us out on dates, haven't. The man who cheats on his wife, I have decided, is most certainly a *bona fide* Sinner. But because on most days I don't prefer to acknowledge, even to myself, that I think any of this disturbing stuff, I continue to parrot the party line that we're *all* Sinners. And, usually, I really believe it.

Just this year, I learned for the first time that not all Christians fool themselves by playing the "sin is sin" game. For example, the Roman Catholic Church is pretty purposeful in distinguishing venial "not as bad" sin from mortal "pretty bad" sin. Though it's not at all politically correct, which I don't think the papacy was aiming for anyway, this strikes me as more honest. The rest of us who pretend to gather all misdoings under one convenient sin blanket aren't fooling anyone anyway. In fact, we'd probably be more truthful if we'd just finally admit that, since sin *does* separate us from God, what we really believe is that some sins have separated certain individuals a teensy weensy bit *further* from the Almighty than others.

Since the Bible says that Jesus was a friend of Sinners, without really designating which *breed* of Sinners, I like to imagine him as a friend to Sinners like me and my friends. I'll tolerate him dropping into an underage frat party as long as he's toting a six-pack of Orange Crush under his arm. I'll look the other way if he wants to chat with a neighbor who I know, for a fact, lies to me about how many minutes she runs on the treadmill. I'll even allow him to carefully, cautiously, mingle with the church elder who fudges on his taxes. I feel far *less* comfortable with my Jesus being sullied by the ones that I've decided are "pretty bad" Sinners. I don't want him milling around the mosque at Ground Zero. I don't want him darkening the doors of a strip club to chat with the manager in the back whom he met at the park where the guy's kids play. I certainly do not want to see him standing by the curb outside the bowling alley on Drag Queen Bowling Night where someone could easily snap a picture of him and post it on Facebook.

The reason I'd like for my Jesus to avoid enjoying these sorts of people and places is because I desperately want to believe that he feels just as uncomfortable and awkward around shameless Sinners as I do. But even though I've scoured the Gospel accounts, I can't find even the tiniest hint that he was driven by the kind of anxiety about otherness, around difference, even about legitimate ritual Religious dirtiness, that would keep him from getting up close and personal with this motley ilk of Sinners.

All of that is my weird baggage.

Hear me: I'm not advocating that every Christian needs to be lining up at X-rated movies or spending lunch hour at a local crack house. For most of us, these special assignments *won't* have our names on them. Occasionally, though, like Jesus, we'll find ourselves in the kinds of places that make the Religious shudder.

## Ticket

Still clipping along at a quick pace, raising a sleeve to wipe my brow, I continued to explain to Jamie, "I think Jesus might even *buy a ticket* just to get in the door of the porn convention to be with all of them."

I really didn't know for sure about the ticket-buying, but I said it with conviction. Though Jamie's expression did not disguise her certainty that I'd now gone off the deep end without a flotation device, I just kept going.

"I think he'd get that ticket scanned, march right into that convention hall, and slowly stroll from booth to booth. I don't think he'd pick up any of the free cherry-scented promotional condoms, but I do think he'd chat with folks. I think he'd look scantily clad women and underdressed men square in the eyes and communicate to them—with his face, his voice, his body, his words—that they were valuable and precious and beloved. I think he'd do the same thing to the leering ones in golf polos and business suits and 'I'm with stupid' T-shirts. Yup. I feel certain of it."

Valuing these individuals, of course, isn't an end but a beginning. Jesus's encounters and conversations with others would be much richer and deeper than a warm expression and a welcoming posture—like the woman caught in adultery, like the woman at the well. It's probably safe to guess that eventually there probably *would* be a "Go and sin no more" moment. But first, there would be grace.

I glanced over at Jamie. Although she'd finally relaxed a little bit once I'd suggested that Jesus wasn't pocketing the free souvenirs, I think she still thought I was full of baloney.

## A Cobbled Deity

I think this fleshy caricature is only alarming to us because we have, naturally, papier-mâchéd together a very thin and hollow incarnate Jesus who behaves remarkably like we do. He feels awkward and tongue-tied around the Sinners who can't, or don't, hide their sin as well as we do. He's quietly concerned about his reputation. Not wanting to appear as if he's condoning sin, he keeps a comfortable distance in public from shameless Sinners. Anxious that their brokenness will expose his own vulnerability, he avoids them privately as well. I feel very confident that this paper-fragile deity wouldn't get within ten yards of Linda's friends' husbands. And while this cobbled character isn't necessarily a *bad* guy by a long shot, I just don't think he's the biblical Jesus. So while this image is a pretty authentic reflection of the person I see every day in the mirror, it seems very unlike the One who closely encountered first-century tax collectors and prostitutes and their motley ilk of friends.

I would love to ask them, though.

# 16

· · · · ·

# report as abuse

Woven into a million different HTML codes online, there's a discreet button that gives readers the opportunity to flag an off-color comment or inappropriate rant. That button lets whoever is hosting or regulating the blog or column know that someone has crossed the line of common decency. It's name?

"Report as abuse."

There was no button, nor would a child even know she deserved to use it, when eleven-year-old Kim V. Engelmann was being barraged by abusive words coming from her mother's angry lips. In her book *Running in Circles: How False Spirituality Traps Us in Unhealthy Relationships*, Kim describes her spiritual abuse in such a way that I understood it for the first time:

> "And you call yourself a Christian!"
> I noticed how tight and white my mother's lips were when she spoke. She was standing on the stair landing above me, hands on her hips.

"You'll never get into heaven with an attitude like that! God knows all the evil thoughts you've ever had about me. Not one is hidden from him."

She continued down the steps, her index finger pointed at me. Her footsteps were heavy, the stubby black heels of her black shoes thudding. The thin pale lips were moving again.

"You'll never please God the way you are. Don't think you won't reap the consequences of your evil thoughts. 'Vengeance is mine. I will repay, says the Lord!'" She was upon me now.

I was eleven. I had vacuumed the house and, according to my mother, not done a very good job.[1]

I felt particularly sad and confused as I read her words. Her father had once been a professor of mine whom I admired and respected. Why hadn't he intervened? Though I wanted desperately to believe that this was a onetime rant, no doubt while he was off teaching some important class, Engelmann's telling reveals that this was anything but an isolated incident.

She continues to voice the words that fell from her mother's cruel tongue:

"If you knew the truth—that I am the apple of God's eye— you would treat me differently!" She was building momentum now, her voice rising. "You are spurning God's chosen one when you look down on me!" The words shot through the air and whizzed at me with their familiar pain.

The culmination was at hand, the consequences imminent.

"You are a hypocrite—full of evil thoughts and lies. A white-washed tomb. Everything you do and say is a lie, and Satan is the father of lies, so you must belong to him!"[2]

Reading along, I decided that *child of a devil* was the first reasonable thing that woman said.

## Origins

That final stab at Kim's tender young heart evokes a similar conversation that Jesus had with Religious folks. After he'd fed the five thousand, Jesus was teaching at the Festival of Tabernacles. Offended by his teaching, they insisted, "You are demon-possessed" (John 7:20). Repeating it several times, they were pretty insistent that he was a bad man possessed by a demon. So . . . it seems like they didn't much care for his teaching.

When Jesus insisted that his Father had sent him, some in the crowd asked, "Where is your father?" (John 8:19).

Whether this inquiry was innocent or pointed, I cannot say, but it quickly devolved into an ugly street-corner "Who's yo' daddy?" sort of confrontation. The crowd questions Jesus's legitimacy and Jesus calls into question the meaning of their Abrahamic lineage. "Who's *your* daddy?!"

Jesus insists, "You belong to your father, the devil, and you want to carry out your father's desires. He was a murderer from the beginning, not holding to the truth, for there is no truth in him. When he lies, he speaks his native language, for he is a liar and the father of lies" (John 8:44).

The larger conversation between Jesus and some haters is clearly where Kim's mom had found most of the ammunition for her assault. And maybe, because the words could be found in the Bible, she even fancied herself as a prophetic word-bearer.

The words that Jesus, an innocent, spoke to the Religious, though, were never meant to be twisted by the Religious to be hurled like sharp weapons at an innocent.

## Don't Read the Comments

This week I heard echoes of Kim's mother's voice when reading the responses to a blog post a colleague had written,

155

which had been posted at Crosswalk. Though I certainly don't equate the harm of a child with the experience of a professional writer who has to tolerate a few ugly comments, the tone and accusations shared similarities.

In a four-part series titled *The Unraveling of a Christian Marriage*, Elisabeth Klein Corcoran shared humbly and vulnerably about the end of her marriage.[3] Specifically, Corcoran answered three questions others had asked about her situation:

Why did you stay in a hard marriage so long?

*How* did you stay in a hard marriage so long?

Why aren't you staying forever?

Fortunately or unfortunately, Corcoran is not in possession of the get-out-of-marriage-free card that so many Christians demand from a woman or man who is divorcing: proof of an adulterous spouse. In an age when men were divorcing their wives for less grievous offenses, adultery, said Jesus, was the only legitimate reason to divorce (see Matt. 5:32). Unfortunately, this means that so many others suffering in emotionally and physically abusive marriages who either choose divorce or are dealt it have gotten the icy cold shoulder from the Religious.

Though those who shamelessly left these comments for Corcoran did so publicly, their names aren't important here. One woman, JPM, who wanted to make sure that Corcoran knew how dead wrong she was for divorcing her husband, explained her concern this way:

If I love my brothers and sisters in Christ, if I love my neighbors as myself, I must love them enough to share with them The Truth.

I suddenly couldn't help but notice how much the capital "T" in "Truth" looks like a hammer.

JPM continues her rant:

> It would be unloving and wrong to leave them with anything
> else. And I must state again that it would also be wrong, when
> I know that God's Word is being used incorrectly and out
> of context, for someone's convenience, to sit idly by doing
> nothing. I care too much for God's people, that is what mo-
> tivates me.

Because I doubt Corcoran experienced the breakup of her
marriage and her family as "convenient," I think I probably
shouldn't comment on how *loving* this is.

TGV, another commentator, offers:

> Every time I get upset, usually it is because I am too easily
> hurt and think too much of myself and become very selfish
> when things don't work out "my way."

Though very loosely draped in first-person language, any
reader knows what is actually being said is, "*You* are upset
because *you* are too easily hurt and think too much of yourself
and become very selfish when things don't work out 'your
way.'"

Yet Corcoran is no proponent of divorce. In her original
post, among a list that includes such orthodox affirmations
such as "I believe God created marriage as a covenant to last
for the lifetime of the couple" and "I believe God would have
wanted my marriage to be healthy and remain intact," Corcoran also includes, "I believe the church is in place to protect and
guide individuals and families in dark, confusing situations."

Not so, says TGV:

> Disagree. The church is in place to bring Glory to God alone.
> Romans 15:6 tells us: The church exists so . . . "that together
> you may with one voice glorify the God and Father of our

157

Lord Jesus Christ." Ultimately, this is the only reason for the church's existence.

A male relative of TGV also gets in on the fun. Based only on the screen names given, it appears MMG is either a brother or an ex-husband. Let's assume *brother*. He offers:

> Even if we are in a terrible relationship, we have not yet resisted to the point of shedding our blood in our fight against the temptation to leave.

*Disagree.* Though I don't know the details of Corcoran's story, the blood of many women—women reading this very blog post—actually *has* in fact been shed, in their marriages.

Repeatedly, throughout the entire online discussion, people *thinking correctly about God* becomes an idol that is being lifted higher than God's own love, grace, and mercy.

MMG continues to insist:

> The reason we all exist is to think correctly about God and to cause others to think correctly about Him as well.

Wait—did God *really* create us so that we could think correctly about him and strong-arm others into the same? Is this truly why we exist? To think correctly about God?

One reader, in my opinion, *did* think correctly about God, when she posted this kind sentiment, "I am for you and so is God."

Please hear that this gracious affirmation could be spoken either by someone who agreed with Corcoran or someone who gently disagreed.

MMG, though, actually disputes the assertion that God is *for* Elisabeth. He wonders . . .

> Is the above comment, "I am for you and so is God," correct because you say it's so, or because God says it's so?

Since I find this transformational reality—that God is for us—on every single page of the Bible, it suddenly becomes inconceivable to me that MMG and I are both reading the same book and referencing the same God. MMG is literally arguing that God is *not* for Elisabeth Klein Corcoran. Report as abuse.

## Silence

When the Religious, like these sincere commentators, speak to and about Sinners in this way, our voices too often become inappropriately *shouty*. And if the volume settings MMG and TGV employ are "shouts," the other go-to volume setting the fervent Religious employ with Sinners is *silence*. Too often, when a kind, gracious "I am for you and so is God" might be the exact way to share the reality of God's steadfast presence in the midst of sin and suffering, our lips suddenly stop moving.

As I read Ann E. Fedeli's adeptly woven memoir, *Are There Skeletons in the Closet?*, I recognized it as a story that was both intimately familiar and deeply important to me.

It is the story of a young woman who, conceiving a child out of wedlock during the 1960s, faces cultural shame surrounding her "condition." Graciously, she is taken under wing at a Florence Crittendon Home for Unwed Mothers.

This is where my own story converges with Fedeli's. Conceived in 1968, as Diana Ross's chart-topper "Love Child" rolled across the radio waves—describing the pain and shame of being born out of wedlock—I spent my last months in utero at Boston's Florence Crittendon Home for Unwed Mothers. Like Ross's protagonist, I was born "illegitimate." Though quickly legitimated, adopted into a two-parent family as an infant, a shame similar to that which the song "Love

Child" made explicit would be, for years, buried in my deepest places. When caregiver after caregiver left me, those who were mine by blood and by adoption and by remarriage, the hiss of shame insisted that I was not worth sticking around for. I was not worth showing up for. I was not worth loving. Because the Religious rarely parse between guilt and shame—between *what you do* and *who you are*—I think this is why all this Sinner business matters so deeply to me. Though now liberated, I was once crushed under the suffocating lie that I was unworthy of love. Today, I simply can't bear for others to either perpetuate it or to suffer under it.

At the Florence Crittendon home, Fedeli is assured by those in charge that once this all . . . passes . . . she will forget and move on to the fabulous life of education or career or marriage that awaits her. The refrain was one familiar to the ears of young women in the 50s and 60s who became pregnant out of wedlock. Though no one ever *purposed* to dupe Ann, what actually happens is that, after "the situation" passes, Fedeli does *not* forget. Some 80 percent of the white, unwed mothers in maternity homes who forked over their children for adoption during the "Baby Scoop Era"—from postwar 1940s through the 1980s when abortion was legalized—were being used as "breeders" for childless couples. Though it sounds like an unlikely conspiracy, it was nonetheless the reality for so many young women who were coached by social workers, with the best of intentions, to relinquish their children.

## Skeletons Exposed

Ann Fedeli had been raised in a Roman Catholic family as one of eight children. She was seventeen when she and her boyfriend conceived. Without being consulted, Ann was sent to a Florence Crittendom home in Washington, DC. The strategy her parents chose for dealing with the situation was to be silent. Siblings were kept in the dark. Family and friends were told that, after visiting relatives in DC over the summer, Ann had fallen in love with the place and would be attending school there to "better herself." Though she longed for a single word of comfort or support, none came.

While she was at the home, Ann's father stopped by for a visit when he was in town for business. During an awkward visit in the home's parlor, Ann writes,

> What I do remember is my silent, anguished prayer that my father would say that he forgave me, that he loved me. I longed for him to take me in his arms and comfort me. Tragically, my huge pregnant belly was too much of an obstacle, and I do not recall that we even touched—not so much as a shake of the hand. My father never let go of his hat.[4]

The echo that still reverberates in Ann's memory from that painful period was her parents' silence. Though she had family members in the Washington, DC, area who might have accompanied her, Ann delivered her child alone, with only medical attendants. Never once did her mother or father—parents of eight children!—ask what the birth experience was like for her. Fedeli reflects, "Maintaining the secret was of the highest priority."[5]

When, several years later, as a student at a junior college, Ann became pregnant again, she secretly had an abortion. At a later boyfriend's suggestion, she sought out a priest to confess. Anxious, Ann entered the confessional and spoke of her sexual sins—illegitimate birth and abortion. The soul-crushing response of the priest: "I don't know what to tell you."

Silence.

When faced with Sinners, our families and our churches have too often chosen a death-dealing silence.

Report as abuse.

Fired up about the judgment of others, we respond with shouts.

Frozen by our fear of others' judgment of us, we respond with silence.

What is most needed in our relationships is a regular indoor voice.

# 17

• • • • •

# live women on display
# and other disturbing
# maladies

Visiting the North Carolina State Fair a few years back, meandering down the midway while my husband snacked his way down Heartburn Alley, I stumbled upon an attraction claiming to feature *The Smallest Woman on Earth*. A large billboard showed a very small, typically proportioned woman standing in the palm of a man's hand. A scratchy recording barked, "Smallest woman on EARTH! ALIVE for your viewing pleasure! Only one dollar! STAY AS LONG AS YOU LIKE!"

Surely, I reasoned, they had not put a human being into a cage for my viewing pleasure. There had to be a catch. It couldn't be possible that anyone would pay money to view a live human woman, could it? Hadn't law-abiding citizens paying money to view folks branded as "circus freaks" gone the way of dusty Main Street shoot-outs between a cowboy dressed in black and one cloaked in white? I was certain stuff like that didn't happen anymore. My mind raced for a solution to the puzzling anachronism. There was simply no possible way that a civil society would put a creature with a human face into a zoolike cage for its viewing pleasure.

## Humanish Creatures

It wasn't the first time I'd had that anxious thought.

I was nine years old and devouring every word of my *Archie and the Gang* comic book. There was an advertisement on the back cover of this particular edition for Sea Monkeys. If I sent $9.99 to the specified address, with my name and address and phone number, they would send me all I needed to breed this odd species of creature, which I wasn't convinced really existed. The copy and illustration suggested that if I just added water, I would grow a family of miniature beings with webbed hands and feet, scaly chests, and small lifelike countenances.

Like the faces I saw around me every day, these cartoon ones revealed bright eyes, a human nose, and toothy white grins. Each Sea Monkey, proportioned just like the body of a human child, had two arms ending in hands with three webbed fingers each, and two legs with webbed-toe feet. The crown of each peachy round face peaked into three prongs, as if each head had been molded into the shape of a jester hat. Flapping behind every Sea Monkey was a long webbed tail.

Though I'd never once seen a live Sea Monkey, I was at once both attracted and repelled. Reasoning that there couldn't *possibly* be Sea Monkeys, I read the ad over and over again, searching for the catch.

Sea Monkeys are everyone's favorite instant pets! While they are very easy to care for, they are an excellent way to teach children about the responsibility involved with taking care of living things.

That anyone would make the claim, in such a reputable journal nonetheless, that adding water to *anything* would produce something with a human face and a full set of teeth like mine haunted me.

## Children's Unfounded Fears

I've since learned that most children have, as I did, a keen inherent sense of right and wrong about these things.

A few years after college, I had traveled across the country to visit my sweet friend Geni and her two-year-old son, Isaiah. I'd made the trip with a life-size dummy named Sonny seated in the passenger seat of my red Ford Escort. Fabricated out of PVC pipe bones, foamy flesh, duct tape ligaments, and smooth attractive panty-hose skin, Sonny was the perfect traveling companion.

Pulling into the parking lot of their Maryland apartment complex, I was excited to introduce two-year-old Isaiah to my life-size doll. Lugging heavy Sonny into their building in my arms, like I might do if I was rescuing someone with a stiff pink terrycloth smile from a burning vehicle, I attempted a knock with the toe of my right boot. As Geni opened the door, instinctively embracing Sonny and I in a big bear hug, Isaiah took a few dubious steps backward. After I'd made the proper introductions, bringing Sonny down to toddler eye-level, he began screaming, "No Sonny! No Sonny!"

It was not at all the glamorous entrance Sonny and I had been imagining for the last two thousand miles.

As soon as Isaiah was distracted, I dumped Sonny in the corner and covered him with a blanket from the couch. As expected, my favorite toddler seemed none the wiser. Yet later that evening as we left the apartment, bundled in our wintry wear, Isaiah turned to the blanketed lump in the corner, waved a mittened paw, and piped with a happy lilt in his voice, "Bye-bye, Sonny!"

The kid was smarter than I thought.

Over dinner, Geni explained to me that there was a Barney costume at a local party store where a friend worked and, although Isaiah loved watching the big goofy purple dinosaur on videotape, he was terrified of the costume. Another little friend of his, she continued, was absolutely petrified of an inflatable Strawberry Shortcake inner tube.

As she clued me in on the mystique of the toddler psyche, I recalled how I'd seen young kids act around birthday party clowns, at once both attracted and afraid. And when children at my church negotiated a new relationship with a beloved teacher who had recently lost her legs, they were curious, intrigued, and also suddenly very shy around her.

And of course, there were the Sea Monkeys.

Whether the *other* is plastic or fleshy or papier-mâché, a child puzzles, sorting through confusing feelings, as she tries to decide whether or not some new other is fully human. The child searches for a category, a file, a box to help make sense of one who's *mostly* human and yet unfamiliar.

Knowing how we instinctively enjoy putting people in boxes, Google Plus has now given adults "circles." It's like a box, except . . . you know . . . *round*. More humane, I think. Dropping someone into a "circle" lets me sleep better at night. Because I feel like they've got company. To quiet our own innate fears about difference, we put people into boxes and circles labeled such things as *costumed, clownish, disabled, redneck, black,* or *foreign*. We're slow to admit it, and never in mixed company, but at a very primal level, we decide who and what is *other* than we are.

Kids just don't hide it.


## Comforting News

While shopping online, I recently came across a banner ad for the Sea Monkeys of my childhood. Though I'd long ago decided that there couldn't *possibly* be amphibians walking around in fish aquariums on two legs or wearing braces or with a pink bow pinned to one of their jester points, I was at last able to confirm it with a few curious mouse clicks.

An enhanced enlargement of one *actual* Sea Monkey—to which I'd never before been privy—revealed that not only were these creatures *not* very monkeylike, they really appeared like something closer to a fungus than anything that would either swing from a tree or walk erect. These tiny swimming organisms—which don't grow beyond three-quarters of an inch—don't look the least bit human at all. They actually look like a fancy twirly shape of gourmet pasta. Sea Pasta, though, would not have aroused nearly as much interest as the purposefully misleading "monkey."

I sleep more soundly now, knowing I will *not* awake to see a slimy, ten-inch-high web-footed humanoid, who's mischievously climbed out of her tank, standing on my nightstand grinning a broad, toothy smile at me. It's shamefully telling how very *much* comfort I take in the fact that these "not-human" creatures do not, in fact, have human features. Like the child who's shut off a Frankenstein flick and flipped on the lights, or the one who's stuck a pair of scissors through a Strawberry Shortcake flotation device, I felt any worries I'd harbored about something, someone, or some inhuman being vivified in my presence had been relieved.

167

## For My Viewing Pleasure

Frozen in front of the attraction claiming to host *The World's Smallest Woman*, my mind searched to fill a similar anxious void. Maybe there was some perfectly reasonable explanation I'd simply not yet imagined.

Maybe, after I'd forked over a dollar, they'd show me a worn sepia photograph of a woman who lived during the days of cowboy shootouts who'd been born with a growth disorder. Perhaps I'd even seen a shot of her before in the *Guinness Book of World Records*.

Or maybe I'd see a little girl—from a Romanian circus family of flying trapeze artists—dressed like a little woman, wearing pearls and eye shadow and high-heeled shoes.

Perhaps, recalling *The Wizard of Oz*, I'd be audience to some sort of electronic projection, watching a lifelike hologram of a typical-sized woman made tiny via illusion.

Or maybe I'd be privy to the dry bones of a once-breathing woman who'd been dug up from under an Egyptian pyramid where, as an ancient novelty, she'd been buried with the kings. I, for one, would feel better about the gawking if I could convince myself her short stature had garnered her some royal privilege.

I desperately wanted any humane possibility among these to be the case.

And though I had never once been tempted to send a single penny to that slimy Sea Monkey address, I was suddenly handing a fair worker my dollar, as if against my will, and winding my way into the attraction.

## Gloria

Before I reached the viewing area, I paused to read some facts that had been posted on the wall about *The World's*

*Smallest Woman.* A photograph showed a short, thick woman who'd been born with a form of dwarfism. To underscore her small stature, she posed with her ten-year-old son who was of typical height.

Her name was Gloria.

Graciously dampened by the jumble of sounds at the fair, the speakers outside continued to repeat energetically, "ALIVE for your viewing pleasure!" Moving forward dutifully to get my dollar's worth, I soon stood looking at the real Gloria. The display featuring the *live* woman was raised up off the ground about three feet to accommodate the gaze of viewers. It was set as a small living room, and sported a small end table, lamp, and a small television. Seated in a toddler's rocking chair was dark-skinned Gloria, available for my viewing pleasure like a waxy figurine at Madame Tussaud's Wax Museum. Her short, meaty fingers knitted a scarf while people viewed her like a common 4-H fair heifer. I noticed that someone savvy, perhaps the Martha Stewart of the carnies, had decorated the minimal living space to look particularly warm and inviting—not at all like a zoo cage—so that idiots like me who had just dropped a buck could soothe our consciences as we wandered out, musing, *Must be nice to sit around all day and watch television. Sweet gig.*

Though our faces were at about the same height, Gloria's eyes did not lift to meet mine. Taped to a metal can, like a tip jar for good service at the neighborhood bar, was a hand-printed sign reading "Donations Welcome."

My busy mind, spinning, stilled itself by zeroing in on operational matters. Why weren't we separated by a thick layer of safety Plexiglas? The guy taking dollars from strangers out front certainly couldn't see or hear what was happening behind him. Not with the boisterous prerecorded barker soliciting curious customers. What if I'd been packing a dangerous weapon in my flowery orange backpack? I would have felt much more comfortable, I think, with a protective barrier. For Gloria, of course.

Horribly embarrassed by my complicity to this dehumanization, I didn't stay long. It was that utilitarian shame—familiar to the privileged, the educated, the white, the tall—that allowed me to feel appropriately bad, like I'd had the right human response to brokenness and injustice.

Though unable to bring coherent words to my lips, I still wanted to share something meaningful with Gloria before rushing out to soothe myself with greasy comfort food. Wriggling up my facial features, I purposed to project an expression that communicated, all at once, "You are a person of value, dignity, and worth. I'm furious you're being exploited. I'm ignorant about who you really are, and what you may or may not get out of this arrangement. I'm having a weird hero-complex moment right now, wanting to grab you out of your rocker, throw you over my shoulder, and run you out of here to safety. And do have a nice day."

It was all terribly confusing for both of us . . . well, at least for me.

So I just tossed a big bill in Gloria's tip bowl, for her and for me, lowered my eyes, and left.

## Outrage and Confusion

Squinting in the bright sunlight, I stumbled out of the exhibit into the loud, sticky crowd of sugared-up fairgoers. Rejoining my husband at the cardiac emergency intersection of powdered-sugar elephant ears and deep-fried Twinkies, I was still very disturbed. Were human rights agencies aware? Where was the fair's next stop and, if Gloria would agree to my weird liberation fantasy, what would she want to do with the rest of her life once I'd rescued her? Would our lives be eternally bound, like a genie and whoever rubs the magic golden lantern to free the genie? I didn't have an answer. As we drove home that night, I felt outraged, ashamed, and confused.

I still do.

# 18
• • • • •

## living with bossy
## (or why we've simply got to
## do more judging)

I'd known Veronica peripherally through friends. We'd participated in a carpool to summer day camp, which is one of my very favorite things: other people driving my children to fun and necessary places. Veronica and I had only shared a smile and a handshake.

A few months after camp, I saw her in the parking lot of the walking trail around a local golf course. She was just getting out of her old Honda Civic. We exchanged pleasantries and commented that we should really walk together sometime. A few days later I emailed her and we set up a date to meet at the trailhead parking lot at 9:05 a.m., after she dropped her daughters off at school.

Pulling into the dusty lot, I pulled my Chevy Suburban in next to her car. Hiding my wallet under the front seat, I hopped out and joined Veronica where she was stretching.

"Hey girl! How you doing?"

Though I know that I should stretch, I never do it unless I'm with one of those overachievers. So I wiggled a little, to make it appear as if I was stretching, and then we hit the trail.

I was telling Veronica how much I hated stretching when she interrupted.

"I just need you to know something," she began.

I replied, "Okay, what's up?"

"I want to be honest. And I just think it's only fair for you to know," she began to explain.

Picking up on her dire tone, I asked, "Do I have a booger coming out of my nose? Is it stuck to the rim of my glasses?"

"No, no," she assured me. "No booger."

"Phew! Okay, what is it?" I asked. "This sounds like the tone you use for something really serious. And we barely know each other. So, what's up?"

Veronica began, "Well, I guess I just need you to know that I don't agree with your lifestyle choice."

"Ummm . . . excuse me?" I asked, thinking she must surely have my lifestyle choices confused with those of someone who's a real Sinner. I do recognize the Religious tone, of course.

"Well, I guess I'm thinking about your cars, your house. And don't you have a few houses at the beach? I guess it just seems a little extravagant. And, although I realize this is a little awkward, I can't help but notice those extra rolls around your middle, Margot. I'm sure it must be really hard for you, bless your heart. I only bring it up because I really want us to be friends. I just need to let you know that I think that material-ism, and overconsumption *on all levels*, is a sin. I love you, but I just felt like I needed to let you know where I stand on this."

"Hmmm . . . interesting," I answered. "Just let me get this clear: you love me. And you want to be terribly sure that I know that you consider me to be a Sinner—"

"Well, we *all* sin."

174

"I know we do, but it sounds like it's important for you to make sure that I know you disapprove of my sins in particular. Does that sound right to you?"

"Well, I just wanted to be sure you knew where I was coming from. So we could be friends."

"Yeah . . . thanks . . . good to know."

## Nutty

In case you're wondering—yes, I made that up. Would we ever *really* do such a weird thing?

With one or two notable exceptions, we really don't. As we're making friends at the park, we don't lead with, "I've had my eyes on you. I think you're a crappy parent, and I'd love to do coffee sometime." If we're youth leaders working with teens who probably party on the weekends, we don't forge a friendship by announcing, "Because I love you, I'm going to tell you that you are an abomination." We don't welcome a pair of new neighbors with a plate of chocolate chip cookies and a stern, "I disapprove of premarital fornication, but do hope you'll join us for a picnic after church on Sunday."

Well, we might do those things, but the people choosing to accept or reject a relationship with us will hardly feel "loved" by our hollow professions of whatever it is that we've defined as *love*.

And yet many of us, conditioned by our Religious subcultures, genuinely believe that such announcements are the requisite way to "love."

## Holy Judginess

I probably shouldn't admit this, but there's a little elf that lives someplace inside me—I haven't quite figured out where

175

yet (elbow? clavicle?)—who whispers instructions to me *all the time*. Let's call him Bossy. Bossy is a nasty little pest. One of Bossy's favorite words is *should*. "You should do this . . ." "You should've said . . ." "You should've been more . . ." "You shouldn't have gone there . . ." Most of these irritated admonitions end with some derogatory nickname for me such as Numbskull or Jarhead.

Most of the time I've got so many other things going in my life that I don't even notice the little brute. I only realize later, after I look at what I've done, that Bossy has been bullying me on the down low.

"Why, again, did I volunteer to chaperone six testosterone-deranged ten-year-old boys on a field trip to an amusement park called Sugar Landing?" Bossy.

"Why did I say I would cohost an eight-hour New Year's Eve party with my Texan friend at a country music bar?" Bossy.

"And how did I end up providing counseling services to this young woman when it's clear to both of us that I have absolutely no affinity for it, no inclination, or absolutely any business doing so?" Bossy!

Sometimes, though, on the rare occasion when the inside of my head is very quiet and still, usually at 2:30 a.m., I do recognize Bossy's weaselly little hiss.

When I'm paying attention, I can hear how this wily little devil tells me that I should judge Special Sinners. He insists that, in Christian love, I owe it to them to speak the truth so that they'll be convicted by their sin. Bossy tells me all the time that the "loving" thing to do is to let them know that what they're doing is wrong. If you're unfamiliar with the procedure, which I pray you are, it means starting—and ending—relationships with heart-hardening icebreakers like Veronica did, with some combination of, "I need to let you know I think your behavior is sinful. But I love you. And God loves you." I don't want to do it. But Bossy says I should.

Honestly, and don't quote me on this, I suspect Bossy has an anxiety disorder. Because he can't bear any tension in my relationship to others, he encourages me to relieve the tension by doing the, "God and I disapprove of your behavior, but we love you" move. That staple of the Religious playbook is what Bossy is always insisting I *should* be doing. Even though I don't like to and don't want to.

I've peeked online, and it turns out Bossy has lots of friends, with too much free time, who post there. These voices insist, "The Bible doesn't say that we shouldn't judge others. If you think it says that, you've read it completely out of context. We should, we should, we should!" In order for us to believe that we're doing it in "love," we convince ourselves that it is our judgment that will lead to a Sinner's repentance.

Without our judgment, Bossy and his human friends insist, they'd be up Sin Creek without a paddle.

## We Really Should Judge

Sometimes when I'm googling, something pops up that tickles my curious bone. So I click. When a recent search for "judge not lest ye be judged" yielded a link that began "The most misquoted verse in the Bible . . ." I couldn't resist. I clicked.

This nutty tirade, by an author who, for no particular reason, we'll call The Judge, was an exhortation to Christians to judge. The Judge was grudgingly willing to concede that God is our *ultimate* Judge, but quickly added that God has commanded *us*, as Christians, to judge others.

The closest thing I found to . . . reality . . . was a passage from Paul's letter to the church in Corinth exhorting Christians to judge sexual immorality in the church. Immediately prior to that passage, though, Paul had been explicit: "I wrote to you in my letter not to associate with sexually immoral persons—not at all meaning the immoral of this world, or the greedy and robbers, or idolaters, since you would then need to go out of the world" (1 Cor. 5:9–10 NRSV). Here Paul has gone to the trouble to say don't *not* associate with Sinners outside of the church. If you're unclear about double negatives, that's as good as saying, "For the love of Pete, of course you will associate with Sinners outside the church! It's *Christian* brothers and sisters who need to be judged."

So it's a little funny that so many Christians and churches are pretty much fine with the Sinners in the pews but have gotten their hackles up about the necessity for Christians to be judging the Sinners out there in the world.

In English we use the word *judge* in two different ways. The dictionary definition suggests the practice of *discernment* about a matter. We discern, or judge, right from wrong. The unspoken addition by advocates of Christian judging is to attach criticism, shame, and blame to that judgment.

The kind of judgment Paul calls us to reject is not wise discernment, but this other shaming kind, "Don't pick on people, jump on their failures, criticize their faults—unless, of course, you want the same treatment. That critical spirit has a way of boomeranging" (Matt. 7:1 Message).

Eugene Peterson's paraphrase of the Scriptures called *The Message* translates Jesus's speck/plank teaching in fresh words:

> It's easy to see a smudge on your neighbor's face and be oblivious to the ugly sneer on your own. Do you have the nerve to say, "Let me wash your face for you," when your own face is distorted by contempt? It's this whole traveling road-show mentality all over again, playing a holier-than-thou part instead of just living your part. Wipe that ugly sneer off your own face, and you might be fit to offer a washcloth to your neighbor. (vv. 4–5)

Our need to criticize the smudginess on someone else's face, I suspect, is propelled by fear. To confirm my suspicions, the online article I'd read by The Judge asked the reader to imagine a world without judgment, warning, "All the prisons would be empty and thieves, serial killers, drug dealers, rapists, and murderers would be loose in your neighborhood."

The announcement is so perfectly absurd, it doesn't even require any snarky commentary from me.

The Judge then offered some closing admonitions . . .

A caring, loving Christian will judge all situations according to the Word of God and call Sinners to repentance.

Because it's caring. And loving.

Obviously, if the church stops judging . . . we will bow down to the devil's wishes to deceive us, our family, and our friends.

Obviously.

God clearly commands us to judge. Why would the command to judge be so vehemently attacked in society?

Me! Me! Choose me! I think I have a hunch.
And finally, the kicker, predicated on intellectual honesty:

If we are intellectually honest when looking at this passage, we will find that it is actually teaching us to judge, not to refrain from judging!

Please: if you *don't* feel like you've just been teleported to Planet Crazy, you might want to look around the room and see where Bossy is hiding.

# 19

• • • • •

# two-headed baby
# born in Brazil

Though something in my gut told me not to click on the headline, curiosity trumped virtue. I have always been wildly curious about multiple births and other birthing anomalies, and the headline promising a two-headed baby could simply not be ignored. With a single click I was staring at a thick, healthy baby who had been born in Brazil with two heads.

Although I'd watched the special cable TV documentary on Britanny and Abigail Hensel, conjoined teens in Minnesota living full lives, my heart fell when I saw these joined babies.

Parents and doctors had been expecting twins, but just moments before delivery doctors realized that they would be delivering conjoined twins. The Brazilian infants, with separate functioning heads, shared a number of vital organs. Each, though, had its own spine and head. Two individuals had been fused in one body.

My mind quickly raced through the possible interventions and outcomes available for these very unique children. Had the mother had early access to medical imaging, I mused, and had the condition been diagnosed earlier, the pregnancy might have been terminated. Many are. I also knew that some conjoined twins could, at a certain optimal point of physical development, be medically separated. I suspected, though, that the multiple shared organs in the Brazilian babies would render this scenario impossible. In some cultures, the twins would be abandoned, exposed to the elements, and left to die. With the high publicity surrounding this case, though, that seemed doubtful.

The most primal, shameful instincts of my gut were to eliminate them, assimilate them, or abandon them. My initial response was not particularly Christian.

## Exclusion

In his prize-winning book *Exclusion and Embrace*, theologian Miroslav Volf gently suggests that, although it's not at the root of all sins, *exclusion* permeates many of the sins we commit against our neighbors.

What?

Volf's hypothesis rubbed wrong everything that seemed sensible to me.

Everybody knows that sin is about *pride* and *disobedience* and *positing ourselves in the place of God*. Now those, right there, are some good sins! To name *exclusion* as being at the root of sin—like not picking Suzie for your kickball team at recess or failing to invite Johnny to your birthday party—just smacked of . . . well . . . tofu, rainbows, and marijuana. I won't lie: at first it sounded to me like this Volf guy might have completed his doctoral work at *Free to Be You and Me* University.

Conceiving sin as the practice of exclusion, claims Volf, "names as sin what often passes as virtue, especially in religious circles."[1]

And with that, Dr. Volf had my attention.

A series of snapshots flooded my mind. I saw a Christian lobbyist fervently fighting to deny civil rights to LGBT folks. I saw a toddler standing with his parents next to a hate placard at the funeral of a gay man. I saw folks from a local church petitioning the city to prohibit a group home from being organized in their neighborhood.

As Volf's claim settled in my mind, I began to realize that his analysis rang true in the stories of just about every Special Sinner who'd shared their story with me. Exclusion, in its various dimensions, has been the fundamental experience of those the church has identified as *other*.

I'm tracking with you now, Miroslav.

## Keeping Sinners at a Nice, Safe Distance

When Tina Anderson was fourteen years old, she was forced to stand in front of her church congregation and confess to a sin that she had no business confessing.

Tina had grown up in Concord, New Hampshire, attending an independent fundamentalist Baptist church there. If she had learned anything at church, Tina had learned to submit to authority. In Tina's church, children submitted to their parents. Wives submitted to their husbands. Everyone submitted to the pastor.

When she was young, Tina's stepfather hit her with a wooden cutting board. When he went to prison in 1989, Tina at last confided to her pastor about being sexually abused by him. And what was the advice of Pastor Chuck Phelps in response to this tragedy? Almost glibly, he assured her that a good Christian forgives and forgets. Whatever she does, she certainly does *not* press charges. In an interview with 20/20's Elizabeth Vargas, Tina said that her pastor forced her to go to the prison to grant her stepfather forgiveness. She went, she says, believing that she was doing what God wanted her to do.[2]

When she was about fourteen, Tina began babysitting for Ernie and Tammy Willis. The following year, claims Tina, Ernie, who had volunteered to give her driving lessons, forced her into the backseat of his car and raped her. One month later, he came to her home and raped her a second time.

The instructions she had received from her pastor were still rattling around in Tina's mind when she was four months pregnant. A Christian forgives and forgets. Tina had refused Willis's offer of an abortion, and also refused his offer to punch her in the stomach as hard as he could to attempt to induce a miscarriage. Finally, she confided in her mother. Immediately Tina's mother called Pastor Phelps.

Tina reported, "I was very scared. I was sure I'd be blamed."

Tina's nightmare continued when Phelps instructed her to write a letter to the congregation asking for forgiveness. In an absurd display of church discipline, Ernie Willis and Tina Anderson were both paraded in front of the congregation on the same day, yet without any hint of relationship between them. First, Ernie Willis stood before the congregation and admitted to adultery. Then, presenting Tina's case as an entirely separate affair, Pastor Phelps read the confession Tina had written as she stood, stained and ashamed, before the congregation.

Instructed not to press charges in order to protect the Willis family, Tina was spirited off to stay with a family she did not know in Colorado. Eight months after delivering her baby, Tina returned to her community. And though she was no longer welcome at the Christian school she had attended, Ernie Willis was still there—chaperoning field trips.

Though Tina—the only player who should have been protected—was *not*, plenty of other people were. Tina's stepfather was protected. Ernie Willis was protected. The Willis family was protected. The church was protected.

What happened to Tina was that she was expelled. She was treated as other, as an object, and as the sin that had infected a congregation and was sent away to Colorado.

We protect ourselves by distancing ourselves from sin and from Sinners.


## Elimination

Sandy was twenty-two years old when her older brother came out of the closet as a gay man. She explains, "He hadn't been intimate with anyone, not even a kiss. He was hurting and wanted comfort and reassurance."

The church Sandy's family attended reacted swiftly by kicking her brother out. When Sandy's mother and sister protested, they were also ousted. Sandy voluntarily resigned her membership. In a small town of three thousand people, word quickly got around about Sandy's brother. Sick of hearing how terrible they were for not being ashamed of him, Sandy, her sister, and her brother eventually moved several thousand miles away. Today Sandy and her siblings are all atheists.

Understandably, I think. Unfortunate and tragic, I know.

I wish Sandy's story was rare. I'd much prefer to believe that her family's story, being mistreated at the hands of a church, was a one-in-a-bazillion anomaly. Sadly, just the opposite is true. Every day, women, men, and teens experience the kind of spiritual abuse suffered by Sandy's brother. In Mel White's *A Stranger at the Gate*, White describes the shameful regularity at which these painful and shameful expulsions occur.

This, I believe Volf would say, is exclusion by elimination. For too long, it has been the specialty of the Religious. A single woman who is pregnant is removed from the small Christian college she attends. A transvestite man is murdered. The child of an exotic dancer is asked not to return to his private school.

## Unholy Obliteration

Exclusion as elimination is not just personal. It is also corporate. Volf points to the shameless brutality in Bosnia and Rwanda. I think of the ugly genocide during El Salvador's bloody civil war. Or the gruesomely effective elimination of the *other* in Nazi Germany.

Recently hearing that a million Indian girls are systematically killed every year because of a gender preference for boys, the same Elizabeth Vargas who helped give voice to Tina's story traveled to India to learn more about this "gendercide." Vargas reports, "The numbers are staggering: 50,000 female fetuses are aborted every month. Since 1980, an estimated 40 million girls are missing through sex-selective abortion, neglect, or murder." In more graphic terms, this means that the ones who are *born* often end up in trash cans.

Ruchira Gupta, a sex-trafficking abolitionist in India, explains, "It's the obliteration of a whole class, race, of human beings."

"The main reason," Vargas explains, "is money. Girls are a financial burden to their parents, who must pay expensive dowries to marry them off." She also explains, "Once married, if a girl's family does not pay a set amount of dowry, she is often beaten, tortured, even burned to death."[3]

For these girls, the consequence for being *other* is, tragically, elimination.

## Assimilation

After World War II had ended, my father-in-law migrated to the United States from Germany as a fourteen-year-old boy. He moved to upstate New York with his recently married German mother and new GI stepfather. In a postwar climate that was cool to Germans, Jurgen Karl Hausmann became American quicker than you can say "apple pie." Most notably, he lost his German accent in no time flat.

Volf names this seemingly more benign side of exclusion as assimilation: "If you can pass as one of us, you'll survive." He describes this kind of exclusion by assimilation in referencing the unspoken "deal" proposed by Claude Lévi-Strauss: "We will refrain from vomiting you out if you let us swallow you up."[4]

The *others* who are willing to play by these rules will be spared.

> If I wear my True Love Waits purity ring, I don't think anyone in my campus ministry will know I'm sleeping with my girlfriend.

> If you look like us, we won't vomit you out.

> If the folks at my church can't handle my Obama bumper sticker, there's no possible way we can actually talk about politics. So I'll keep it zipped.

If you sound like us—or at least don't sound *not* like us—we'll tolerate you.

A father tells his son, "Oh I'm fine if you have a boyfriend, just don't bring any of that into my house."

If you pretend to behave like us, we won't spit you out.

The deal Lévi-Strauss references is the whole reason that many gay, lesbian, bisexual, transgender, and transsexual folks choose to stay in the closet—keeping their orientation secret—rather than publicly acknowledging this part of their identity. The ones who have grown up in so many churches have, ironically, survived by pretending to be *other* than who they are: literally, *other* than *other*. They were told, or discovered, or intuited that to continue to be included in the group, to prevent being vomited out, they'd need to give the appearance of belonging.

And, for the most part, they were right.

## Abandonment

Finally, Volf names a third form of exclusion:

> It is exclusion as *abandonment*. . . . If others neither have goods we want nor can perform services we need, we make sure that they are at a safe distance and close ourselves off from them so that their emaciated and tortured bodies can make no inordinate claims on us.[5]

Folks who experience divorce in the church often report suffering this type of abandonment. Many find that they're no longer included in many of the invitations they received when they were "half of a couple." Others suffer much more explicit abandonment.

Stacy had suffered, for years, in an excruciating marriage. When she'd asked for help from those at church, she had received trite platitudes.

"Pray more."

"Submit to God."

"You're not supposed to be happy, you're supposed to be holy."

After years of dysfunction, Stacy finally staged an intervention to ask her husband to deal with his harmful behavior. He was not interested in change.

When Stacy ultimately decided to divorce, she experienced abandonment from the church. Her sister and brother-in-law severed their relationship with Stacy, refusing to speak with her. Not only did Stacy's pastor insist that her decision put her salvation in peril, but he also called the pastor at the new church Stacy began attending to warn them about her unwillingness to submit to the church's authority.

Stacy shares, "Other people in my community do not speak to me. They treat me in a less than loving way on a regular basis. People gossip about me and I hear about it."

Rather than experiencing the church's warm embrace at the moment when she most needed it, Stacy experienced abandonment.

## Expel

Like the placental tissue a woman's body expels following birth, we expel those members whom we've decided are not useful to our social or Religious agenda. Or those who are perceived threats . . . seen as cancers to be removed or eradicated.

The state in which I live is now considering passing legislation that would, among other things, exclude members of gay couples from legal entitlement to the benefits they're now receiving from their private employers. Though private employers would have the *option* of extending these benefits, employees would have no legal recourse should they be denied. The legislation's passage would mean both that current employers would be less able to recruit talented qualified workers—read *Sinners*—and it would also reduce the number of viable businesses that would be willing to locate here. Under the thinly veiled Religious guise of "protecting families," we are on the verge of legislating that Special Sinners must find another state in which to live and work. If this legislation passes, we will have, in effect, begun the systematic process of excluding Special Sinners from our midst. And, largely, we will have done it under the veil of Religious virtue.

Like Volf said.

Though he wasn't talking about local politics in my state at all, Volf warns:

> Sin is here the kind of purity that wants the world cleansed of the other rather than the heart cleansed of the evil that drives people out by calling those who are clean "unclean" and refusing to help make clean those who are unclean. Put more formally, sin is "the will to purity" turned away from the "spiritual" life of the self to the cultural world of the other, transmuted from spirituality into "politics" broadly conceived, as Bernhard-Henri Levy puts it in *Dangerous Purity* (Levy 1995, 77).[6]

I realize that those are some big fancy words but, recognizing our impulse to cleanse the world of the *other*, they do ring true. And for too long we've done it in the name of Religious virtue.

Denying civil rights to gay folks, we claim to be "protecting families."

Stealing the land from its natives, we "created a free nation."

190

Unleashing apartheid, we were "honoring God's natural ordering."

Employing eugenics, we were "purifying the human race."

Committing genocide, we were "creating a stronger society."

And we've dared to call all of it *virtuous*.

## A Different Way

Enter Jesus. Who beelined toward the ones his culture excluded as sinful. And ironically, in his signature topsy-turvy method, his intimate presence among them functioned to identify their *exclusion* as sinful. Rather than sin functioning to infect him, his presence served to expose their unholy exclusion for what it was.

Volf explains:

> In the Palestine of Jesus's day, "sinners" were not simply "the wicked" who were therefore Religiously bankrupt (see Sanders 1985), but also social outcasts, people who practiced despised trades, Gentiles and Samaritans, those who failed to keep the Law as interpreted by a particular sect (Dunn 1988, 276–80). A "righteous" person had to separate herself from the latter; their presence defiled because they were defiled.[7]

No one in first-century Palestine *didn't* know how Jesus should have been behaving. The Religious knew and the Sinners knew. Namely, he should have been keeping his distance from Sinners who could defile him. Had he been more politically conniving, he would have avoided them entirely. Yet Jesus's presence among Sinners confirmed their intrinsic value and defied their culture's and our culture's concept of sin.

191

Since he who was innocent, sinless, and fully within God's camp transgressed social boundaries that excluded the outcasts, these boundaries themselves were evil, sinful, and outside God's will (Neyrey 1988, 79). By embracing the "outcast," Jesus underscored the "sinfulness" of the persons and systems that cast them out.[8]

That is called *turning the tables*, I believe.

## Embrace

Our human instinct, upon encountering the *other*, too often is to eliminate, to force assimilation, or to abandon. Those were the impulses that, unfiltered, sprung from my own heart when I saw a digital photo of the recently born conjoined twins.

The Brazilian mama who bore them gave them the names Jesus and Emmanuel, meaning "God is with us." If they are anything like their namesake, the arms they share will reach out, toward some *other*, in embrace.

# 20
• • • • •

## moving toward people
## who really matter

As I was heading into my final year of junior high, our student council president-elect was Ellen Highstone. If there was a shiny sparkly star at our junior high, Ellen was it. Blonde-haired and blue-eyed, energetic, visionary, and inordinately intelligent, she was the perfect person to be president of the student council.

In a much less publicized race—possibly uncontested?—I had been elected president pro tempore. Though the responsibilities of the position weren't entirely clear to me, then or now, I was under the impression that if the president and vice president were to get hit by lightning on the same day, I would at last wield some sort of authority.

Elections had been held in the spring for the forthcoming school year. Returning home from a summer of fun at Camp Miniwanca, I was informed by my mother that Ellen had called and invited me to a party. Though I'd been to lots of birthday parties, I'd never been to a party-for-no-reason party. Because I wanted to know Ellen better, I was delighted by the invite. That a little bit of her social capital might rub off on me wouldn't hurt either. It wasn't even September yet, and the privileges of holding office were already rolling in.

After being greeted by Ellen's sister and mother at the front door, I clumped down the basement stairs to join the other guests. Peeking at the early-comers who'd beat me there, I was immediately struck by the social . . . breadth . . . represented in the Highstone underquarters. There was the star of the school play. There was the cute smartie cheerleader that everyone envied. There was the math wiz that no one envied. There were the other student council officers. And, of course, there was Ellen.

Three years before John Hughes's classic film *Breakfast Club* shone a spotlight on the array of youthful humanity that could be found in the Chicago suburbs—winners and losers, goths and jocks, geeks and freaks—Ellen Highstone had gathered just such an ensemble in her suburban Chicago basement.

Because that kind of thing usually only *does* happen in the movies, my wheels began turning to figure it out. Why would someone with so much social capital risk it by associating with some of these . . . non-winners?

Was it a calculated political move? No, she'd already been elected.

Had she invited some of these folks out of pity? Her evident enjoyment of them didn't suggest that she did.

Had she invited them there as some sort of a cruel, vicious prank? Were we about to be punked? Per her goodness, the odds seemed unlikely.

Was it possible that she really didn't know what the rest of us knew intuitively? Could Ellen Highstone have undergone a weird social lobotomy, by which she was missing the part of the brain—so highly developed in the rest of us preteens—that decides in a millisecond whether or not others are *worth* knowing?

It seemed, in that moment when I descended the stairs, as though she might have. Since, to my knowledge, no one at the party was given a wedgie, shoved into a toilet, or otherwise humiliated, it seemed like she invited us all there because . . . she wanted to.

Ellen was just a confident kid who wasn't worried that associating with the lot of us would drain all her cool points away. Not only did her radical hospitality speak well of her— and cause me now, three decades later, to want to emulate a thirteen-year-old girl—it also said something about her guests.

It said, to me anyway, that we were *worth* knowing.

## My Peeps

I can't help but compare Ellen's motley crew to the cadre of people with whom I spend my time today.

Most are women within about a decade or so of my own age. Most are employed. A number of them are married. A bunch are parents. Most are heterosexual. They're well-educated, well-groomed, well-dressed, and well-housed. I'm not aware that any have criminal convictions. Most of them are people of faith who care about justice. So . . . basically . . . they're a lot like me.

It's my understanding that, as a species, as a people, this is how we are. We sort of clump together in homogenous little tribes. Throw us all into the same cafeteria or school or city or workplace and we'll still clump. There's something soothing about others like us, who mirror back whom we know ourselves to be.

Does it mean that I think other people aren't worth knowing? Of course not. That's just silly.

Or is it?

Part of the offense of Jesus's presence among identified Sinners was this very thing. That lepers were ostracized outside of city limits, or that menstruating women were untouchable, or that tax collectors dined amongst themselves, or that folks with physical disabilities were believed to be Sinners upon whom tragedy had rightly fallen suggested that these ones really weren't *worth* knowing. They shouldn't be touched. They didn't need to be afforded respect. And to top it off, they deserved what they got.

Jesus's presence among these precious ones sent a radical and disarming message to those who'd be just as happy to brush them off like unwanted mosquitoes. The message, the same one I'd encountered at Ellen Highstone's party-for-no-reason, was that each one was *worth* knowing.

Had Jesus *only* rubbed shoulders with the Religiously respected, or morally righteous, or alpha males, or attractive fitness instructors, there might have still been this lingering question in the minds of many: Am *I*, with my sin and the ugly I try so hard to hide, worth knowing? Am *I* worth loving?

Case after case, person after person, Jesus continues to answer yes. Yes. Yes. Yes. Yes. You are *worth* knowing.

## Waiting

Because there are so many days when I can barely believe that of myself, there are just as many days when I doubt it of others. Especially suspiciously loitering others.

I was driving downtown, kids buckled into their car seats, when we stopped at a red light. At the intersection stood a shady-looking young man.

I can think of only one reason for standing around on a street corner. To my judgie mind, the only *good* reason you need to lurk at a street corner is to cross the street. Possibly you're poised to help a tourist who's lost his or her way, or wave a large stop sign while helping children cross, but more often than not, if you're not wearing a neon orange vest, the only good reason to be on the corner is to cross the street.

One of the clues that this young man was a no-good, drug-dealing hoodlum, of course, was that, when the traffic light allowed, he wasn't crossing the street. He simply . . . lurked. His apparel, posture, and gaze only added to my suspicion that he was not a confused tourist amnesiac crossing guard. Though I didn't spend more than a moment noticing him, it took only a millisecond to silently pencil in a checkmark to the box in my head beside the words, "Not Worth Knowing."

While I was behind the wheel, so busy with all the judging, my three-year-old son, Rollie, had noticed the young man too. And in the same way I'd projected my ugly onto the man, Rollie would project his innocence.

Also silently noodling on why a corner-dweller wouldn't cross the street, Rollie eventually broke the silence by musing aloud, "Maybe he's waiting for his *daddy* to come."

The unexpected possibility was entirely disarming. Suddenly squeegeeing the grimy window through which I saw the world—a world in which some folks were worth knowing and others weren't—Rollie saw only someone who was *worth* knowing. He saw someone who was loved and who was worth taking home.

Immediately I imagined a concerned dad slowing his sedan down to a stop. Hopping out of the car, scurrying around to the other side, he gave his boy a warm hug and threw open the passenger door.

Now, had I driven by and witnessed *that* scene, I would have known, intuitively, that this boy was worth knowing and worth loving.

"Maybe," I answered Rollie, suddenly softening. "Maybe he's waiting for his daddy."

## Unlikely Movement toward Sinners

My friend Kerry is a minister in the inner city of Dundee, Scotland. He cares deeply about effective practices of grace, faith, and social justice. He's a coleader of a church in Dundee that's committed to loving God, sharing life, and serving generously. Kerry is also the executive director of *Signpost International*, an organization that focuses on community transformation by listening to the voices of people living in poverty. Kerry is one of these types I love who's all about living a life of love for those on the margins.

Kerry tells the story of meeting a local man we'll call Sam, who'd lost his son in a tragic car crash. Although Sam wasn't a Christian, he'd sought out Kerry in order to ask him to perform the funeral service for his son. That heartbreaking beginning became the seed that led to a relationship of trust between Kerry, Sam, and Sam's wife. And each time they got together, Sam, curious, would ask about Kerry's faith. This speaks so well of Kerry, doesn't it?

One day, Kerry's phone rang. When he answered, Sam was on the other end, asking if Kerry would be willing to meet with some of his buddies. Intrigued and confused, Kerry asked why.

With unbridled enthusiasm, Sam reported, "I want you to tell them about God!" he said. "I have tried to tell them what you have been telling me and now they all want to meet you!"

Flattered and pleased, Kerry happily agreed to meet them all for a beer and conversation at the local rowing club. I guess "rowing club" is like . . . a thing . . . in Scotland. Although it sounds sporty and chic, "rowing club" is actually less like a golf club or tennis club and more like a man cave.

Hearing the good news, Sam enthusiastically added, "It's going to be a great night. There's even going to be strippers!"

## Second Thoughts

Kerry drew a deep breath. A Religious insider, albeit an edgy one, he knew something about ministry in a small community. He knew how people talked. If one set of eyes spotted him at that club on stripper night, Kerry's reliable reputation would be in jeopardy. Though he had no reason to believe that he'd be inordinately tempted, Kerry simply knew that he couldn't go.

"Oh!" he quickly said. "If there's going to be strippers then I can't come."

The phone went dead.

Kerry humbly explains, "I have many regrets about what I said on the phone that day. I did not say what I said because I felt in any moral danger, but because I feared what other Christians might think and say. My need to 'control' my reputation took precedence over showing love and acceptance to a group of guys on a genuine search for God."[1]

Though Kerry made many attempts to heal the relationship, the friendship was never restored. In reflecting on this event, and his behavior, Kerry reasons, "Mud sticks."

He knew that, in a small community, any smear on his Religious reputation would be with him a good while. And as he reflected, Kerry became increasingly aware that mud stuck to Jesus too. The company of the Sinners Jesus enjoyed was no less muddy and grimy and reputation-infecting than that of the strippers and scallywags in Dundee. And for Jesus, it wasn't like he was once spotted in a sketchy rowing club because he made a one-time decision. His friendship with Sinners wasn't accidental either, as if they were strewn across the road and he just couldn't get away fast enough. Rather, time and time again, the pattern of Jesus's life was to move *toward* Sinners and not away from them.

In fact, in moving toward Sinners, Jesus chose to sacrifice a reputation of Religious *rightness*. Did you catch that? He was willing to scrap the appearance of Religious rightness—the one that Kerry and I both value very much—in order to move toward Sinners in love.

It is a movement that is, from my vantage point, entirely counterintuitive. In fact, just the thought of doing that thing guaranteed to put me on the outs with respectable Religious folk feels like a small death.

## Insiders and Outsiders

When people talk about *insiders* and *outsiders*, I have a very clear opinion about the group in which I'd prefer to be numbered. I want to be an insider. I don't care if it's a ministry or a speaker's club or a gossip circle, I would still prefer to be included rather than excluded. I'd rather be an insider than an outsider.

Last night, my friend Amey Victoria was giving me a ride to Raleigh Correctional Center for Women. Amey Victoria and another friend, Sarah, who was working at the prison, were teaching a course on spiritual biography that included students who were incarcerated at the facility. About half of the class members were women from the facility and half were not. Sarah had invited me to teach a lesson on "voice" in writing. Although, when she asked, I didn't really *know* a lot about voice in writing, I agreed anyway. By the time we were battling Raleigh's rush hour traffic on eastbound I-40 though, I'd learned enough that I could teach something without being terribly embarrassed. Mediocre nonembarrassment is sort of my own personal standard of excellence.

As we drove, we were discussing some of the experiences she'd had with the women at the prison. As she spoke I started to pick up prison lingo like "solitary" and "canteen" and "privileges." In fact, I slowly realized that "inside" indicated something or someone *inside* the prison, and that "outside" meant the whole rest of the world that wasn't stuck *inside*. (I really am more clever than most people often guess.)

Prison, of course, quickly turned everything I had ever known about *insider* and *outsider* quite literally inside out. Insiders were no longer the privileged few in some prestigious inner circle, and outsiders were most certainly not desperately pining away to become insiders. Rather, in this new economy of out-ness and in-ness, being an *insider* pretty much stunk.

The same type of careful attention and energy I give to securing my insider status in the *regular* world matches the kind of effort and energy women on the inside put into being granted their *outsider* status. They speak respectfully to people in power. They are purposeful about doing all the "right" things. They stay clean and sober. They show up for bunk checks. They take their meds. And just as, in my world, I have to distance myself from outsiders a little bit in order to sidle up to the insiders, the women inside who are gunning to become outsiders have to separate themselves from the *insiders*.

I mentioned this was upside-down crazy, right?

## An Unlikely Plan

Upside-down crazy is exactly what people thought about the kingdom Jesus ushered in. For centuries Jews had been waiting for a king like David who would *finally* clean house. But in the unlikely kingdom established by the Prince of Peace, citizens were being asked to turn their cheeks to get a second slap, pick up their crosses, and lose their lives. Ick, right? In this new inside-out kingdom, power was exchanged for weakness and privilege for sacrifice. Clearly, prison-insiders and prison-outsiders was an equally mind-bending concept for me.

I was interested in hearing from Amey Victoria what her involvement with the prison had been like. She told me that she'd started as a student in the class—as an outsider—and that, at Sarah's invitation, she'd taught two courses since then. She explained that originally Sarah and her friend Jonathan had wanted to offer the course in a maximum security prison, but that they had not been granted permission. Prison officials had reasoned that the opportunity to participate in the writing class made sense for women at RCCW, who all had less than five years of their sentences to be served, but that it would be wasted on women with longer sentences and no reentry into the community in sight, who would continue to waste away at the more secure facility.

The fact that they'd been flatly denied access, though, had not diminished the hopes of Amey Victoria and Sarah. As we neared the prison, my generous driver shared with me their dreams for the future.

"We're trying to break into the maximum security prison," she explained, as if it was the most reasonable thing in the world.

That funny sentence made me giggle a little bit.

The satisfaction, and even delight, Amey Victoria experienced with that announcement was entirely evident. She was an outsider after all, allowed inside for just two hours a week. It quickly became evident, though, that she was living in some other sort of reality than the one in which most Americans dwell. In Amey Land, the women in the prison really were the insiders Jesus loved, and she actually spent time and energy scheming how to get even deeper in, moving closer to the ones Jesus loves.

And though the instinct of most of us is to move as far away from Sinners as we possibly can, Amey Victoria and Sarah simply could not get close enough. At the prison that evening, I witnessed the gratitude of the women who were incarcerated. That Sarah and Amey Victoria, and a host of others they'd roped into their shenanigans, would be chipping away at the gates of the prison, sweet-talking officials into giving them more access to those on the inside, had blessed the women inside.

It had surprised the insiders a bit because, more often than not, the Religious would just give Sinners like them the once-over and then slowly take a cautious step back. Sometimes we'll do it purposefully, but most of the time we're not even aware of the ways in which we distance ourselves from harmless Sinners who pose absolutely no actual threat to our health or well-being.

Whether or not there are concrete walls and barbed wire fences separating us, we keep our distance from Sinners because we feel uncomfortable in their presence. Figuratively, more than literally, we don't want to catch what they've got. We certainly don't want to threaten our good reputations by having anyone assume we condone their behavior. So for the Religious to move *toward* identified Sinners, without wielding either a hateful placard or a gospel tract, or wearing a T-shirt announcing "I'm Not with Them," is, for many of us, the exception rather than the rule.

For Jesus, though, it's the rule.

It marked him and it's meant to mark us.

# 21

• • • • •

## double the strategy

As a rule, I try to avoid vastly oversimplifying that which is necessarily complex.

To make broad sweeping generalizations about groups of people—the Chinese, the fundamentalists, the gays, the Republicans—is like slapping a one-ingredient FDA nutrition label on a bag of trail mix. When we do it, we blanket an assortment of tasty goodies in an opaque bag that reads simply "pretzels" or "marshmallows." And while it may be partially true, it disguises and hides what's really there. Because any group of people is bound to have its share of fruits and nuts, typically no good can come from the opaque packaging and singular sticky label.

Sometimes, though, it does.

Specifically, boiling a type down to its most fundamental ingredient is useful—when it illumines, rather than darkens.

Recently, my friend Heather's sweepingly succinct reduction did this very thing for me. "To vastly overgeneralize," Heather summarized, "one segment of contemporary

American Christianity is fine with defining people as Sinners but not okay with being a friend; the other segment is fine with being a friend but not okay with calling people Sinners."

She is so dead-on, isn't she? In a broad, sweeping way.

If I were strangely forced to further reduce these warring elements—if that's even possible—I'd be tempted to use a fat black Sharpie to label the two packages of people she describes as *Truth Mix* and *Love Mix*.

If you ripped open a serving of Truth Mix, you would certainly expect to find some Religious conservatives in the bag. And while there would be a handful who could be called fundamentalists, more would be mostly moderate. Not only would folks in this bag be naturally comfortable identifying others as Sinners, they would, by virtue of their shared orthodoxy, be *obligated* to do so. To many in this Truth bag, "love"—the way it's been used by the Lovers, anyway—sort of sounds like a dirty word. Real love, they maintain, can only be practiced in the light of truth.

If you tear into the Love Mix, you'd certainly find some of those stereotypically liberal granola types. And while there would be a handful who would push the outer-left bounds of orthodoxy, more would be mostly moderate. Having more of a seemingly natural bent toward reaching out to, rather than identifying, Sinners, they would in fact, by virtue of their shared commitment to orthopraxis, be *obligated* to do so. To many in the Love bag, "truth"—the way it's been used by the Truthers, anyway—sort of sounds like a dirty word. Real truth, they maintain, can only be preached in the light of love.

American Christianity, Heather is saying, is what happens when, after the party, a tired host dumps the leftovers from the two separate mixes into one bowl.

## My Problem

I've come to suspect that part of the reason I find myself caring so very deeply about this business is that I have a salty-sweet hand in each of these mixes.

Recently, I was a guest at a beautiful Nashville farm property belonging to a popular Christian recording artist. When the other guests were talking about life on the road as a well-coiffed Southern Gospel musician or a gospel-announcing evangelist or a tattooed Christian rock star, I could only smile and nod, very aware that I was, technically, not counted as one of their own.

At the end of that same week, I was volunteering at a chic local entertainment venue where North Carolina AIDS Awareness was raising money by hosting drag queen bingo. Whether the other guests were talking about the single lesbian bar in Durham, or gay clubs in neighboring Raleigh, or the empowerment that comes from celebrating the feminine through drag, I could only smile and nod, aware that I was, technically, not counted as one of their own.

Clearly, over my "I love Jesus" stockings, I've got a muddy cowboy boot on one foot and a sparkly six-inch, size-twelve stiletto on the other.

Now, I realize that when a lot of people identify themselves with this hand-in-both-bowls, foot-in-both-worlds effect, they know—or at least suspect—that others will think *more* of them. When they donate millions of dollars from their vast family fortunes to both HIV-AIDS research *and* to missionaries translating the Bible into the language of a random remote people group, we like them even *more*, don't we?

For the record, I don't for one moment expect my confession to play out that way.

Not only do I feel equally dorky and out of place in both groups, as members of either will attest, but the people-pleasing part of me is equally desperately afraid that conservative folks at my church will find out I enjoy the company of despised Christian liberals and that my gay friends will find out I write for *Focus on the Family*.

I'm nothing if not a complete mess.


## So Different Than Me

Thank goodness there is Jesus, who is nothing like me or *any* of my friends.

Jesus was so concerned with pleasing his Father that he was entirely unconcerned with pleasing people. That he purposefully offended and/or surprised every last person, and not just half of them, never ceases to intrigue me. Those of us who long for our values to be determined by him, rather than by either culture or religion, are being drawn into an unlikely third way.

Miroslav Volf warns:

> It would be a mistake, however, to conclude from Jesus' compassion toward those who transgressed social boundaries that his mission was merely to demask the mechanisms that created "Sinners" by falsely ascribing sinfulness to those who were considered socially unacceptable (*pace* Borg 1994, 46–61). He was no prophet of "inclusion" (with Johnson 1996, 43f.), for whom the chief virtue was acceptance and the cardinal vice intolerance.[1]

Jesus, claims Volf, did something else entirely. Instead,

> He was the bringer of "grace," who not only scandalously included "anyone" in the fellowship of "open commensality" (Crossan 1991, 261–64; Crossan 1994, 66–70), but made the "intolerant" demand of repentance and the "condescending" offer of forgiveness (Mark 1:15, 2:15–17).[2]

To identify the ways Jesus is just like me and my friends, which the salty Truthers and the sweet Lovers could both do, would be to miss the point *entirely*. I've become convinced that there's much more to be gained by identifying the ways Jesus is entirely different than either one of our Religious proclivities. The days I'm leaning right, it's alarming that Jesus scandalously includes any and all into fellowship. The days I'm leaning left, it's equally scandalous that Jesus offers forgiveness for the sins I'm just as happy to sweep under the rug and invites transformation.

Volf continues to explain:

> The mission of Jesus consisted not simply in *re-naming* the behavior that was falsely labeled "sinful" but also in *re-making* the people who have actually sinned or have suffered misfortune. The double strategy of re-naming and re-making, rooted in the commitment to both the outcast *and* the Sinner, to the victim *and* the perpetrator, is the proper background against which an adequate notion of sin as exclusion can emerge.[3]

Jesus didn't have just *one* strategy, like too many of us do; he had a *double* strategy. Which is . . . like . . . twice as much strategy.

Recognizing how our binary thinking and labeling excluded people unjustly, he renamed that which had been *falsely* labeled unclean. Time and time again he ripped off the FDA *unclean* label and, in word and deed, included those who were outsiders. No food was unclean. The flow of blood from a woman's body was not unclean. No one's sin caused a man to be born blind.

> The mission of re-naming what was falsely labeled "unclean" aimed at abolishing the warped system of exclusion—what people "call clean"—in the name of an order of things that God, the creator and sustainer of life, has "made clean" (cf. Acts 10:15).[4]

Renaming would most certainly have made the Truthers, in his day and ours, more than a little uncomfortable.

Jesus's other strategy was remaking. If something was truly unclean, he made it clean. Folks who were possessed by unclean spirits, or caught in the snares of wrongdoing—whether to benefit themselves or just to survive—were forgiven and transformed.

"The mission of re-making impure people into pure people," claims Volf, "aimed at tearing down the barriers created by wrongdoing in the name of God, the redeemer and restorer of life, whose love knows no boundaries."[5] Remaking would most certainly have made the Lovers, in Jesus's day and ours, more than a little uncomfortable.

As complementary members of the same nutty mix, we've both, technically, on different counts, been *right*. Doggedly maintaining our rightness, though, has failed to transform us into the likeness of Jesus. Ironically, that will only happen when we acknowledge our wrongness—the ways we've failed to rename or to remake—and follow Jesus into the less-comfortable way. Volf concludes,

> By the double strategy of re-naming and re-making Jesus condemned the world of exclusion—a world in which the innocent are labeled evil and driven out and a world in which the guilty are not sought out and brought into communion.[6]

If we don't join Jesus in this renaming and remaking, we only perpetuate the kind of exclusion he came to abolish.

# 22

•••••

# Fred Phelps funeral

Pulling a pile of envelopes and unwanted catalogs out of our mailbox, I quickly rifled through the stack. Scouring the contents for mail that I deemed "good"—writing contracts, personal letters, notices that I'd won a large sum of money—I found none. I did, though, whisk two envelopes out of the stack and dropped them into the small garbage can near our front door before my husband could see them. Had he laid eyes on either of these envelopes, he would have been *completely* disgusted with me.

It all began, as so much mischief does, quite innocently.

I had accidentally seen a photo online of Fred Phelps's hate group boycotting a military funeral with their horrible damnation placards. By now you know how I can be with these salacious temptations. Though I know now I should have just clicked on to the next atrocity in the daily news, for whatever reason, on that day, his monkey business simply *demanded* an authentic Christian response. After all, the

New Testament offers plenty of advice on enemy-loving. These recommendations include, but are not limited to: extending kindness, being merciful, doing good, and even lending money.

For whatever reason, the one that came to mind that day was a *different* injunction, the one about heaping burning coals on your enemy's head. Quite frankly, that one really appealed. Googling "heaping burning coals," I quickly located the reference in Paul's letter to the Romans. You can imagine my disappointment in discovering that this heaping coal advice was just a colorful way of saying extend kindness, be merciful, and do good.

With actual flammables off the table, I tried to imagine how goodness might triumph over evil in this particular instance. So, naturally, I decided to organize demonstrators to picket at Phelps's own eventual funeral.

## Funeral Procession

While my inner marketing manager was already composing signs that said, "Who's in hell now?" and "Surprise!" a little cartoon angel on my right shoulder cautioned against it.

Instead, what I began to imagine was a radical display of *love* at that blessed event. Slogans began coming to mind as quickly as I could write them down.

> God actually doesn't hate fags.
> God loves fags.
> Whoops! God probably doesn't say "fags."
> God is love.

It was like a spiritual gift I never knew I had. Or one that God even gives. And since I didn't want to be the *only* one looking like a lunatic on the evening news, I realized I needed to rope in some like-minded friends.

I immediately messaged a national figure I thought might be interested in this monkey business. I knew him well enough to be Facebook friends, but not well enough to know his wife's name. This guy, I thought, might actually have the skills and ingenuity and public platform to get this little campaign off the ground.

And since no one builds this kind of a weird tower without counting the cost, I priced last-minute plane tickets to Phelps's home city, and decided I would be willing to spend the money in order to demonstrate God's love in the face of twisted evil.

Within minutes, I had shelled out actual dollars to commandeer the domain name www.FredPhelpsFuneral.com as well as the matching email address. The email address, of course, would be a drop box for people to send in their own clever placard slogans. Then, whenever I felt like making signs, I'd have them ready for game time.

## Dubious Peter

So this is kind of how it went with my husband, Peter, when I called him at work.

"Hello, this is Peter."

"Hey babe, can you just send me a quick email at fred phelpsfuneral@email.com to make sure it works?"

(Uncomfortable judgie silence.)

"What have you *done*?"

Though I'd been imagining myself as some radical akin to Oscar Romero, his tone made me suddenly feel more like Lucy Ricardo.

"Well, it's kind of a long story . . ."

213

I knew exactly what my cautious spouse was thinking in that moment. He was imagining the actual Fred Phelps finding out about my little campaign and staging a protest in our town, on our street, in front of our house. I knew he was thinking that my little shenanigans had put our children at risk of life and limb. And though I'm not quite the worrier he is, I had to admit that if it was a slow week for Phelps, one when a lot of his archenemies didn't die, I could sort of imagine the same thing.

## Through Wind and Rain and Sleet and Snow

It wasn't long after registering the domain name that I began receiving snail mail addressed to FredPhelpsFuneral. Even more disconcerting were the ones that had the wherewithal to include spaces: Fred Phelps Funeral. The first one I received, quickly tucked away in a pile of work papers where my husband couldn't find it, was a solicitation for a Yellow Pages ad. And though I didn't pay these vultures any money for the two-page spread, I was still afraid that the listing would end up in the phone book. And honestly, I don't know that it hasn't.

My favorite solicitation, to date, has been the free assortment of preprinted holiday greeting cards in shiny reds, greens, and golds. Because I'm sure everyone wants to know they've been remembered during the holidays by their friends at Fred Phelps Funeral.

## RLC

I was still pretty pumped about this business when I posted a little piece about it at *Red Letter Christians* blog. It seemed like just the place to drum up some enthusiasm from fellow activists. One reader's humble comment, though, sort of stopped me in my tracks.

He wrote:

> It would make for a good publicity stunt, but I doubt that the Phelps family would feel loved. Letting the family mourn in peace by not bothering them or silently paying our respects and wishing the family well at the procession might have a greater witness.

I hate it when people like this are so right.

It is so much more pleasurable to love the kid who gets extorted by the class bully than it is to love the bully. But if Jesus's words about loving your enemy are to be believed (see Luke 6:32–36), then they include Fred Phelps and family. The apostle Paul's letter to a church that probably loved as poorly as I do also confirmed this:

> Love is patient, love is kind. It does not envy, it does not boast, it is not proud. It does not dishonor others, it is not self-seeking, it is not easily angered, it keeps no record of wrongs. Love does not delight in evil but rejoices with the truth. It always protects, always trusts, always hopes, always perseveres. . . . Love never fails. (1 Cor. 13:4–8)

I cannot even tell you the last time *not* dishonoring others ended up on the evening news.

## Will

Will Campbell, friend of racist rednecks, was also a friend to other Sinners. I don't mean that in the way that we sometimes romanticize the Sinners with whom Jesus was friends. I don't mean that Campbell was a friend of someone who collects taxes at the IRS, and complained about his job. I don't mean he handed a bottle of water to an ex-prostitute at a homeless shelter, being careful not to make physical contact with her. I mean that just as Jesus was friends with grimy Sinners, Will Campbell was friends with grimy Sinners. Specifically, Campbell befriended members of the Ku Klux Klan.

When I first learned this, I wanted it to be something other than what it was. I hoped that maybe he had just gone to high school with some of these jokers and then tossed back a single beer with them at their twenty-five-year high school reunion. I wanted to believe that Campbell used his Mississippi drawl to cozy up to these folks at a coffee shop so he could immediately tell them how dead wrong they were. I wanted to believe he was neighbors with them, and maybe lent them the occasional hedge clippers, but that their relationship didn't go beyond such requisite pleasantries. Searching, scanning for any plausible explanation, I wanted Campbell to be like civil rights activist Ann Atwater, from Durham, NC, who strangely befriended a Klansman named C. P. Ellis in such a way that he was eventually transformed. The last thing I wanted to believe was that Campbell treated unrepentant, active members of the Ku Klux Klan as human beings created in God's image.

While the stories I made up about Campbell allowed me to force together radically incongruous pieces of a jigsaw puzzle, the record shows that Campbell genuinely cared for these folks. He married them. He buried them. He visited them while they rocked on their front porches, and he spent time with them when they were in prison.

Quite frankly, I found Campbell's liberality, which had threatened and offended so many on the right for years, to be quite unpalatable. Campbell, unlike so many of us, didn't seem to have the good sense to distinguish between the worthiness of the oppressed and the worthiness of the oppressor. As Frye Galliard reports in *Race, Rock and Religion*, Campbell simply explained, "Mr. Jesus died for the bigots as well."[1]

While it may have been technically true, instinctively I want to shout out, "No! No! Don't you know? He died to free the oppressed, not the oppressors! Haven't you even read the Bible?!"

In a 1976 interview with Dr. Orley B. Caudill, for the Mississippi Oral History Program of the University of Southern Mississippi, Campbell reflected on the nature of these relationships: "I didn't deliberately go out and say, 'I am going to have a ministry to the Ku Klux Klan,' as the Ku Klux Klan." In Campbell's mind, these ones whom I had vilified as monsters, the same way they had done to so many, were just people. To Campbell, pale people who wore white masks were no more or no less people than dark-skinned ones who were hosed down in the street by police officers. To Campbell, every individual, created in the image of God, was worth knowing and worth redeeming.

When Caudill was interviewing Campbell in 1976, Campbell shared a recent insight. "You know, this is strange. It's been a long time since I got a hate letter from the right. Now they come from the left."

Eventually, from the right and from the left, Campbell had enemies.

Right there is where Will Campbell and I part ways. Because while I like to identify with the man who stood for justice, I am simply in no mood to receive hate mail. It may be related to a very primal fear of abandonment. For whatever reason, I am happy enough to make my way through life mostly enemy-free. Thus far, I have. As far as I know, anyway.

## Not Me

When I'm eating at the food court of the big warehouse store in my town—cash, check, or debit only!—I like to peruse the shoppers who are pushing their oversize carts from the checkout line to the exit where, receipt in hand, they wait to be released to their vehicles. Specifically, I keep my eyes open for people I know.

As I enjoy my cheesy pizza, I like to connect with the mom from my kids' soccer league. I enjoy chatting with the pastor from across town. I'll wave at all the people from my neighborhood who shop where I do. I'll count up all the ones from my church. Though I'm really not an extrovert and would rather floss my teeth with barbed wire than be at a party, I find these brief, upbeat social encounters to be altogether manageable. At the end of the day, all these pleasantries sort of confirm, in my mind, that I'm a pleasant sort of person without too many enemies.

Honestly, I can't think of one. More often than not, I'm courteous and kind. I avoid conflict more often than I cause it. I can't think of one person who'd name me as their arch-enemy. I'm not saying they're not *out* there, these enemies who might despise me and wish me harm. I'm simply saying that, at this point, they have not yet come forward to identify themselves. As far as I know, I'm enemy-free.[2]

I'll tell you why this works out so well for me: enemy-less, when I read Jesus's clear Sermon-on-the-Mount injunction to *love* my enemy, I'm sort of off the hook. I won't lie: I find the whole set-up altogether satisfying.

In my deepest places, though, I've sort of suspected for a while—in part because Jesus wasn't addressing the United Nations—that Jesus surely had something else in mind (besides warring states) with enemy-love.

## Ian

Having absolutely no idea how smug I've been about having no enemies, my neighbor Ian recently shed some needed light on the whole canard.

Last week my family had dinner with our neighbors. Though we don't do this nearly often enough, we enjoy the company of Wendy, Ian, and their children very much. Because Ian is the director of Duke University's Franklin Humanities Institute, I attempt to keep from being intellectually intimidated by reminding myself that his kids poop in their diapers and don't pick up their dirty socks and vomit in the middle of the night just like mine do. I know it's sort of pathetic, but it actually helps a little.

The four of us were wrestling together to understand Jesus's clear injunction: "But I say to you that listen, Love your enemies, do good to those who hate you" (Luke 6:27 NRSV).

Native English speakers like myself read Jesus's admonition as "love your enemies." For generations we've heard the Greek word (*exthros*) χθρος—as in "love your χθρος"—translated as *enemy*. For better or for worse, it's the best English word we've got.

Latin, though, has several words that might have been used to translate the Greek, χθρος, we've learned as *enemy*. One of those words is *hostes*. At dinner, Ian was really fired up about the Latin translation of the New Testament Greek word we know as *enemy*. He's sort of a word nerd. But because he's a socially aware word nerd, he wasn't about to bore us all with his own little fascination-of-the-moment that hinged on an ancient translation.

"Why don't you tell them," Wendy urged, when our conversation provided a natural entrée. It was kind and proud, the way she might have urged one of her children to present a finger painting to the dinner-guest audience.

Sheepishly at first, Ian explained, "The Latin *hostes* has the shading of a 'public' enemy or 'state' enemy."

Becoming excited, he began speaking a little faster.

"It's an enemy possessing sovereign state power against whom another state can legitimately wage war, but whose standing as an equal sovereign power it needs to respect—with a fully attached set of rules for how war can be conducted, prisoners treated, and so on."

He said it with such effective enunciation and emphasis and facial expression that I actually understood him.

But *hostes*, explained Ian, was not the word St. Jerome used to translate the Greek *exthros* in the fourth century. The other Latin word for enemy is *inimicus*. Literally, it means not-friend. *Inimicus*, Ian told us, refers to one's private enemy. And while this person could be a personal adversary—a competitor who wants to destroy you in business, or the cheerleader who stole your boyfriend—it could also be one who is simply radically *other*.

Ian enthusiastically continued, "In translating 'love your enemy' as *diligete inimicus vestros* in the Vulgate, Jerome is asking us to understand the massive scope of Christ's love command—that it is directed not just to the neighbor or even the respectable enemy, but to all those we believe are most utterly unlike, antithetical, and inimical to us."

He had the happiest look on his face, more like someone who had just won a big stuffed teddy bear at the state fair than someone who was describing something as unsavory as enemy-love.

## Back on the Hook

"Vulgate, Vulgate. . . ." I searched my memory banks to retrieve whatever little information might still be there from my Intro to Church History seminary class. When I had learned about Jerome and the church fathers and the Vulgate almost twenty years earlier, I could hardly imagine how they would ever pertain to my everyday life. Shortsighted, I know.

I could even justify my not-caring with a superior air, and say, "In the unforeseen event that a real textual emergency should arise, I can peek at the Greek or the Hebrew myself. Please don't confuse me with some middle language that no one speaks anymore unless you're patiently explaining the root language of an unwieldy word to a panicked seventh grader in the Scripp's National Spelling Bee."

For almost two decades it didn't matter. For nineteen years I was so right about how wrong—maybe even criminal—it was to use up space in my head knowing things about a Latin Bible that even the Roman Catholic Church had scrapped in favor of people worshiping in their own native tongues.

Then suddenly, one day, it mattered.

*Inimicus* puts me back on the hook because, although I'm not at odds with any sovereign nation-states, everywhere I look are folks who are utterly unlike, antithetical to, and inimical to me.

Since I'm square into my middle years, there are the young and old ones.

Since I'm beige, there are all the rich shades of brown and tan.

Since I'm female, there are all the males.

Since I'm North American, there is an entire globe full of non–North Americans.

Since I'm English-speaking, there is everyone else who's speaking other languages.

Since I'm mostly able-bodied, there are the ones whose
limbs and brains and bodies don't always cooperate the
way they might prefer.

Since I'm heterosexual, there are all the folks who identify
as decidedly *not* heterosexual.

Since I'm Christian, there are all those who do not identify
as Christian.

Since I'm free, there are those who are enslaved and oppressed and bound.

As of this draft, I'm a generally law-abiding citizen.

Faithful in marriage, so far.

You see how I could go on all day with the folks who are
inimical to me?

## Vestros

You can too. That's what's so wily about the unlikely admonition Jesus drops on us like an atomic bomb. The one who is
*inimicus*, radically other, will be different for each one of us.

The Latin *vestros* means "your."

I emailed Ian a few days after our lovely dinner to get some
more info on this business.

Humbly, Ian explained, "The *vestros* part of the command
is in that sense as important as the emphasis on 'love' and
'enemy.' It is our most despised enemy, the *inimicus vestros*,
the one most antithetical or inimical to 'us,' wherever we are,
in whatever moment, in whatever place, in whatever situation (political, social, personal) that Christ is asking us to
love: the despised, abandoned, outlaw, threat to 'us,' whose
utterly inimical, completely unprotected being he took on
himself on the cross."

Suddenly seeing Jesus nailed to the wood, in my mind's eye it was as if he were hanging on a coat hook like they have in elementary schools. And if Jesus was on that hook, under the weight of the despised, then I could no longer *not* be on the hook with him.

# 23

• • • • •

# condoning, condemning, and loving what is

I'm not going to lie. When I saw my husband propped up in bed one night reading Oprah's Book Club pick *Loving What Is*, by Byron Katie, I thought it looked kind of silly. The way he explained it to me was that we find psychological and emotional health as we're able to accept things as they really are. For example, rather than having a nutty screaming reaction when my child's nutty screaming drives me crazy, I'd choose instead to just *notice* that my child was screaming like a nut. I wouldn't come all unglued and start freaking out myself. Rather than wishing my child wasn't upset—and being upset by it myself—I'd just *notice what is* and then sort of let it pass by.

Yeah, right. Like that would ever happen.

I couldn't possibly see how my husband's latest psychological solution, this voodoo magic mind game, was going to really work on the ground. I didn't see how choosing to love what *is*—like my kids' arguing, hitting, disappointment, disobedience, and distress that I find so . . . distressing—was going to make our lives any better. I thought it sounded ridiculous and I let him know it.

## Maybe Not *So* Bad

Then, one day, a wise Christian therapist whom I completely trust mentioned the same book.

She began by sort of testing the waters to see if the word "Oprah" would make me froth at the mouth while smoke billowed out of my nostrils and my head spun in circles. When it didn't, when I assured her I was open to the possibility that I might learn and grow from something that had been endorsed by Oprah, she mentioned this *Loving What Is* approach by Byron Katie. When she explained it, I thought it was pure genius.

"Loving what is" just means that instead of desperately wanting some situation to be different than it actually is—which, since I usually can't control it, only causes me distress, anyway—I accept it for what it is. As I do that, when I stop the relentless thoughts that insist *This has to stop*, or *I can't bear this*, or *Why are they trying to destroy me?*, I don't have to be distressed by it. What *causes* my upset, apparently, is me wanting a situation to be different than it really is. When I accept what is, as I just notice what's happening, I don't have to get freaked out by it.

A few examples . . .

Hmm . . . I'm noticing that the child who refused to stop playing Legos long enough to fill a water bottle before this soccer game, when I suggested he do it, is now standing on the sidelines desperately thirsty. And miserable. And crabby. That's so interesting.

Hmm . . . I'm noticing that when I asked my daughter to turn off the television she threw the remote across the room. That's interesting.

Hmm . . . I'm noticing that because someone in my family monkeyed around with the computers and printers, I am no longer able to print the important document I need to print right now. Very interesting.

If you're a highly evolved, emotionally mature person, this is probably how you behave all the time. You don't let yourself get ticked off and unglued by small inconsequential things. Because I do, however, the difference between the groovy, psychologically sound, spiritually healthy response and me blowing up and screaming at ~~someone~~ everyone is really quite striking.

## Radical Shalom

I didn't decide that this approach was good stuff just because Oprah said so. Let's be very clear on that. Rather, I decided it was pure genius because it embodies the radical shalom that I *witness* in the person of Jesus.

His mother's pressuring him to magically produce wine at a wedding party? Shalom.

Crowds of sick people pressing in to be healed? Shalom.

Pharisees getting up in his grill, calling him a glutton and a drunkard? Shalom.

Crowd picking up rocks to stone him? Shalom.

One of his friends freaking out and cutting off the ear of someone who was in the wrong place at the wrong time? Shalom.

Any one of these things would have sent me over the edge. But not Jesus. Somehow he is able to manage all manner of craziness because he seems to begin from a starting point of accepting what *is*. He doesn't endorse all of it, of course, but he also doesn't explode or whine that things ought to be other than they are.

It's all really very counterintuitive.

## Whine, Threaten, Scream

A lot of us have a hard time accepting what is because we desperately want things to be other than they actually are.

Of course we do.

- If we're moving through traffic behind someone who is driving very slowly and poorly and dangerously because she's texting America's next great novel, we want her to shape up and speed up.
- If we've been waiting on hold for thirteen minutes with our cell phone provider because we don't know the password to access the voice-mailbox that has the message giving us the password that would allow us to access our voice-mailbox, we want things to be other than they are.
- If we're single and we'd like to be in a relationship, or if we're married and would like to be out of a relationship, we want things to be other than they are.
- If we're on standby at the airport, waiting for a spot on the last flight home, and can tell from the "cleared" screen that we've made it up into second position, and we suddenly drop down to fourteenth position, we want things to be other than they are.

So we curse. Or we cry. We whine. We threaten. We scream.

On one of these flights that I barely slipped onto, I sat next to a man who clearly wanted things to be other than how they were. In regular intervals, as we waited on the runway, he would look up from the book he was reading, sigh loudly and deeply, and swivel his head around for no other reason than to give a flight attendant the stink eye. Then he'd drop his gaze back down to his book. Four minutes later he'd be repeating the loud-sigh swivel-glare routine. It wasn't just on the runway, either. He continued to do so after we had commenced hurtling through the atmosphere. I tell you, this guy was wound tight. And in case it wasn't obvious, I found his aggravation to be completely aggravating.

So then I took my own deep breath, let out a long (quieter) sigh, and practiced the Byron-Katie-but-Really-Jesus magic trick.

*This guy seems really upset by the delay. Hmm . . . isn't that interesting?*

It totally worked, people.

Now, I'm not pretending I could practice this if it had been my *husband* in the seat next to mine, but with this stranger I did not have to experience one more moment of distress because of his distress.

Sometimes we can get "triggered" like this by the behavior of others that we believe to be sinful.

Perhaps my husband is the perfect example. It is no secret that he sins regularly by transgressing the posted speed limit on our residential street. Whether he's driving my dorky mini-van or is behind the wheel of his super cool jeep, he'll quickly accelerate from parked to terrifying nonresidential speeds. One neighbor, on the block south of ours, has alerted the police. Another neighbor one block north gives me regular reports on my husband's transgressions. Not only are there small children living across the street from us, there are three residing under our very roof.

So I am faced with a choice.

I can feed bitterness and resentment by perseverating on thoughts such as:

*This is so dangerous.*

*He's going to kill someone.*

*What will the neighbors think?*

*Why does he have to be such a* moron?

*I thought we agreed we were going to* love *our neighbors, not kill them. I must have misunderstood our agreement.*

Or, I can notice, *Hmm, how interesting. There he goes again.* (And be secretly happy when he gets stopped by a cop, like he did last week.)

To say Jesus was a "friend of Sinners" means that he wasn't embarrassed, the way I am, by what anyone had done.

## Twisty Logic

For me to accept that my husband has sped recklessly, or that my child has just pummeled his brother, or even that plenty of folks used to think the earth was flat, isn't to condone them. I'm not waving a checkered flag on the front porch or giving my son candy for every black eye he can inflict or blogging about how flat the world is. Rather, for me to accept that these events and ideas have existed in time and space is simply to acknowledge reality. It's to notice what is and *accept* it.

While I'm flattered that someone Religious thinks my opinion matters, the truth is that neither my seal of approval—nor my seal of disapproval for that matter—are the least bit efficacious. Case in point: the behavior of the offspring who live in my household. While I'd love to think that by condemning underage drinking, plagiarism, promiscuity, second-generation reckless speeding, or any other of a host of social ills, I could prevent just one of them, it simply is not the case. Were I to register my condemnation (aka "opinion") with the local magistrates, announce it from a pulpit, and wear it printed on a neon T-shirt, I still would not be responsible for the choices made by others.

If it actually were the case that my acceptance of the riff-raff, my presence among them, was an implicit endorsement of their behavior, then Jesus is not the man a lot of us think he is. According to this line of thinking, he's proprostitution, proextortion, proadultery, progluttony, prohypocrisy, prodrunkenness, and prosyncretism. The twisty logic says that if you "accept" something, you necessarily condone it. Even if you don't.

Whether or not Jesus condoned or condemned the behavior of Sinners, he did *accept* it. He recognized what was, without signs of anxiety or distress when others failed to behave the ways he thought maybe they should.

I tell you, this wasn't Byron Katie's brainchild. Rather, freedom from distress—freedom *to* love!—was Someone Else's idea entirely.

# 24

•••••

# the moment Ted Haggard
# went home justified

The same way that I know pretty much how the people in my home will behave—if the Wii is broken, or if I serve a really bad meal, or if someone loses twenty bucks—Jesus's audience knew how Pharisees behaved and how tax collectors behaved. They also knew how they might have prayed.

The crowd knew who the Pharisee was. He's the holy one, marked by righteousness.

They knew who the tax collector was. He's the unholy one, marked by sin.

The Pharisee, said Jesus, prayed, "God, I thank you that I am not like other people—robbers, evildoers, adulterers—or even like this tax collector. I fast twice a week and give a tenth of all I get" (Luke 18:11–12).

"Yup," his listeners might have said, nodding to themselves, "I've seen this episode. I know how this one goes." Whether those listening were Pharisees, which Luke sort of suggests by describing some folks in the crowd as "some who were confident of their own righteousness and looked down on everyone else" (v. 9) or whether they were grimy Sinners, that prayer would have rung true.

Jesus has pulled them in.

While the Pharisees might not have ever stooped down to listen to the prayers of a bowed one who wouldn't even look up to heaven, they would certainly have agreed with the praying tax collector in Jesus's story. When he prays, "God, have mercy on me, a sinner" (v. 13), they would have nodded in agreement that he was, indeed, a sinner.

Jesus has pulled them in deeper.

But wait! Unexpected twist ending! Jesus surprises every last person in the crowd by announcing, of the tax collector, "I tell you that this man, rather than the other, went home justified before God" (v. 14).

Lest they think him possessed by a demon, which first-century crowds were actually wont to do, Jesus added a little explanation for good measure: "For all those who exalt themselves will be humbled, and those who humble themselves will be exalted" (v. 14).

Jesus might as well have said, "The earth isn't flat or round. It's actually in the shape of a pyramid." Or, "I have sixty cousins who live in space."

Everything the Religious and the Sinners thought they knew about how the world worked just got turned upside down and inside out.

Their eyes were opened.

## Maggoty Insides

Jesus knew how these guys operated because he'd spent time with them. In fact, Luke tells us that previously Jesus had been teaching and healing when a Pharisee invited him to lunch.

And while it hardly seems, to me, that a stodgy Pharisee could have been half as much fun as dining with the Sinners, Jesus willingly joined him and kicked back in the Pharisee's crib.

As they settle in to eat, the Pharisee notices something that troubles him: Jesus doesn't participate in the ritual hand-washing before the meal. To be clear, for the Pharisee, this isn't about bacteria. It's about Religious custom. As Jesus is fully *aware* of the custom, it almost seems like he might have wanted to provoke this guy. As was his way.

Eugene Peterson's paraphrase of Scripture helps us hear how Jesus might have responded using the vernacular of our day.

> I know you Pharisees burnish the surface of your cups and plates so they sparkle in the sun, but I also know your insides are maggoty with greed and secret evil. Stupid Pharisees! Didn't the One who made the outside also make the inside? Turn both your pockets and your hearts inside out and give generously to the poor; then your lives will be clean, not just your dishes and your hands. (Luke 11:39–41 Message)

"You're one thing on the outside and another on the inside." Jesus wants them to see who they really are, and then extend mercy.

> I've had it with you! You're hopeless, you Pharisees! Frauds! You keep meticulous account books, tithing on every nickel and dime you get, but manage to find loopholes for getting around basic matters of justice and God's love. Careful book-keeping is commendable, but the basics are required. (v. 42 Message)

"Yes, you're meticulous about your law-keeping, but you've neglected justice." He wants them to see who they really are, and then practice justice.

You're hopeless, you Pharisees! Frauds! You love sitting at the head table at church dinners, love preening yourselves in the radiance of public flattery. Frauds! You're just like unmarked graves: People walk over that nice, grassy surface, never suspecting the rot and corruption that is six feet under. (vv. 43–44 Message)

"You're full of death and you don't even *know* it." He wants them to see who they really are, and be vivified. Jesus continued, now including the Religious scholars who'd been listening in.

You're hopeless, you religion scholars! You load people down with rules and regulations, nearly breaking their backs, but never lift even a finger to help. (v. 46 Message)

And on it goes. He wants them to see who they really are, so that they can be *for* others.

You're hopeless! You build tombs for the prophets your ancestors killed. The tombs you build are monuments to your murdering ancestors more than to the murdered prophets. (v. 47 Message)

"You pretend to honor the prophets, but you're really honoring your families. You are, essentially, honoring yourself." Again and again, Jesus wants them to see who they really are.

Luke says that when Jesus finally left the table, the Pharisees and Religious scholars went into a rage.

It's a charming picture, no? It's a snapshot of the thing Jesus has just described. Though they managed to hold themselves together in Jesus's presence, when Jesus leaves, their true colors—furious orange, raging red, plotting grey, and maybe even envious green—are revealed.

Though Jesus held up the mirror of veracity, they remained unable to see who they *really* were.

## Hypocrite?

Sadly, today there is no shortage of titillating scandals involving high-profile people of faith who present as "hypocrites." One of the most infamous in recent memory involved Ted Haggard, pastor of New Life Church in Colorado Springs. At the time, Haggard was also the leader of the National Association of Evangelicals.

In November of 2006, Haggard was publicly supporting Colorado Amendment 43, which would ban same-sex marriage in the state. Disturbed by Haggard's duplicity, escort and masseur Mike Jones came forward to allege that Haggard had, over the course of three years, been paying him for sex. Jones had known that Haggard was married and had no interest in disrupting his personal life. That would have been really bad for business. It was only when Jones discovered Haggard's public persona, specifically the one lobbying for antigay legislation, that he was moved to come forward and reveal the relationship.

The former gay prostitute accepted Haggard when he presented himself as a Sinner who knew he was a Sinner. He took issue, though, with a Sinner who posed as a saint.

Jones explained, "I had to expose the hypocrisy. He is in the position of influence of millions of followers, and he's preaching against gay marriage. But behind everybody's back [he's] doing what he's preached against."[1]

As several of Jones's allegations proved to be true at Haggard's own eventual confession, Merriam-Webster could, legitimately, have inserted a photo of Ted Haggard next to the entry for "hypocrisy." I *still* wanted to know, though,

how Haggard measured up according to Jesus's own definition of hypocrisy, as reflected in his conversations with
first-century hypocrites: Did Haggard *see himself* as he
really was?

Before the scandal broke, Haggard's loud public support
for Amendment 43, without any sort of personal transpar-
ency, suggested he didn't. But, like the Pharisees who dined
with Jesus, he was given a unique opportunity when Mike
Jones shoved a mirror in his face to take a good long look at
himself. Would he look into that mirror and see what was
really there, or would he drape it with false images?

Initially, no doubt stunned and confused, Haggard denied the allegations, saying, "I did not have a homosexual
relationship with a man in Denver . . . I am steady with my
wife. I'm faithful to my wife."[2] In fact, he claimed he had
never met the accuser.

Eventually, though—either from a contrite heart or to
extend a little bone to the mad media pit bull salivating for
his flesh—Haggard would publicly confess that *some* of the
allegations were true.

And right there was the golden moment of opportunity.
There's the moment that Jesus describes the story in Luke 18
of two men who went to pray. In the moment that counted,
one man, a Pharisee, denies all wrongdoing. The other, a
Sinner, a disreputable tax collector, admits to his utter depravity and need for mercy. This, says Jesus, is the one who
went home justified. The moment Jones's allegations became
public was Haggard's moment to decide.

Though it must have been uncomfortable, Haggard was
given the opportunity to end his hypocrisy and say, "You
know what? I'm a mess. I really am. Guilty." In that holy
moment Haggard could look into the mirror and recognize
who he really was.

Instead, Haggard chose to offer to the public—whether we bought it or not—implausible denials

... that a concierge had recommended the services of the seedy former male prostitute.

... that he'd gone to the first encounter for "just a massage."

... that, tempted, he *bought* crystal meth, but then threw it away.

I don't know if the excuses are true. While they may be true, they seem weak. They sound and smell and feel and look like masks. From the little I've gleaned about human nature, by virtue of incarnating it, I suspect Haggard was and still is doing the best he could and can.

After several years had passed, in January of 2011, Haggard came out as being bisexual. Because Haggard didn't really "owe" that to the public, that moment could have happened just as authentically, privately, with his wife or family. As it was, he chose to make it public.

Whether public or private, with one's spouse or with one's God, that kind of rigorous honesty *matches* the picture Jesus paints of the man who went home justified.

# 25

● ● ● ● ●

## until the fat lady sings

A grandfather sits by the side of his grandson's bed to read to him from an old, dusty book. The story is called *The Princess Bride*. Though the boy is a little put off, initially, by a bit of kissing, he continues to listen dutifully, wooed by the promise of pirates and giants and swordplay. And although he's not heard this particular story before, he mostly knows how these things go. The good guys win and the bad guys lose. The end.

This story has been going on for quite a while when the boy learns that evil Prince Humperdinck has tortured Westley, the story's hero, to the point of death. Westley's acquaintances Fezzik and Inigo—who had previously been unsuccessful at killing him—have found him, expired, in the Pit of Despair.

"He's dead," observes Fezzik.

Inigo mourns, "It's just not fair."

Disturbed, the boy in the bed interrupts the story, "Grandpa, Grandpa, wait. Wait, what did Fezzik mean 'He's dead'? I mean, he didn't mean dead. Westley's only faking, right?"

This was not the story he'd signed up for.

The grandfather calmly answers, "You want me to read this or not?"

The boy presses, "Who gets Humperdinck?"

Toying with him, the grandfather says, "I don't understand."

Riled up now, the boy persists, "Who kills Prince Humperdinck? At the end. Somebody's got to do it. Is it Inigo? Who?"

"Nobody. Nobody kills him. He lives."

"You mean he *wins*?" Disgust drips from the boy's lips. "Jesus, Grandpa! What did you read me this thing for?"[1]

While I was a bit startled they'd dropped the J-bomb in a family film, it was an oddly appropriate outburst over a dead hero who was about to be resurrected.

The boy knew how a good story was supposed to go. A princess caught in the grip of death is unable to extricate herself. A hero comes along to rescue her. Released, the life of the liberated one then becomes a function of the redeemer. The princess marries the prince and they live happily ever after. The end. Storybooks and animated versions of *Cinderella* and *Snow White* and *Sleeping Beauty* had convinced the boy that this was the pattern. This was the arc of a good story. The boy could simply not reconcile a dead hero and a living villain. It suddenly became a story without meaning.

## Our Temptation

Christians can be tempted to do the same thing in relation to the stories of Sinners. Rather than recognizing that—this side of the grave—a person's story is continually in process, we recognize only a snapshot that *appears* to tell the whole story. Unable to calculate how death could possibly give way to life, or how a gracious God could possibly redeem someone we've identified as a hardhearted Sinner, we experience anxiety. When an individual's story does not unfold as we might expect, we abandon hope. We abandon Sinners. Childish, we demand, "Jesus, what did you read me this thing for?"

Like the boy, when we experience dissonance in another's story we can give way to despair. But for those who trust in a God whose mercy is inscrutable, there is another possibility. For these, dissonance actually generates *hope*. Hope is birthed as individuals relinquish their uncertainty and fear to place their trust in a story greater than the one they see. When presented with an image of a dead hero or an entombed princess, they *recognize* the moment as a single frame in the midst of a much larger moving picture. As they put their trust in the *author*, and not the actor, they are able to bear the tension created by a story that is, as yet, unresolved.

For instance, when I walk past the guys on the corner selling drugs, I frame it as if that single snapshot is the whole story. This kind of vision leads me to heave a sigh of resignation and say, "It's so sad these lives are being wasted. This is a sad story."

The second kind of vision, though, the one that is open to the possibility of another ending we cannot yet see, says, "This is *one frame* in a moving picture. I wonder what might possibly come next in this story?"

Do you see the difference? One way of looking at a scene is to assume that the entire story is contained in one still moment. The other way is to recognize the moment as just one frame in a larger narrative whose ending is, as yet, unknown. To trust in the Author, who's also the producer, is to make room for the possibility of redemption.

## Emily

Admittedly, it is not always easy to maintain hope in a God of transformation when scene after scene in a loved one's story points to a disappointing denouement. My friend Emily describes the heartache of her faithful mother when transformation was not as she expected.

"My mom first met Jessica through a program that paired Christian suburban women with women transitioning out of prostitution who lived in Phoenix. Jessica has been in our lives ever since and calls my mom and dad her parents. Jessica's two teenage kids spend a lot of time with my parents and consider them their grandparents."

Fifteen years have passed since Emily's family first met Jessica.

"Anyway, I know my mom has a hard time with the role she has played in Jessica's life because she sees so little transformation in her, even after all these years of mentoring, praying for her, providing material resources, and treating her like a daughter."

Emily's mom has witnessed chapter after chapter after chapter of despair.

Emily explains, "I think my mom expected Jessica to be transformed in a very obvious way through all of the investment. There are significant changes that have occurred in her life, like stopping prostitution, getting off drugs, getting and keeping a job at a gas station, getting off welfare after many years of subsisting on it, and getting good health care for her AIDS."

From my vantage point, that sounds like a good show.

"However," Emily continues, "there are so many things about Jessica's character, spiritual life, and basic personhood that really bother my mom. I think it is becoming more pronounced as my mom sees how Jessica is negatively impacting her kids. I get the sense that my mom feels disillusioned, wondering about the ultimate value of her role in Jessica's life and questioning how much she has done."

It's hard to hold out hope of a satisfying conclusion when chapter after chapter suggest otherwise.

Emily grieves for her mother, because she's seen what an extraordinary impact her mother *has* had on Jessica's whole family. She laments, "Mostly, I want Mom to accept in a deep way that she is not and never was responsible for any transformation in Jessica's life, that she was just called to love and be faithful in this relationship that God gave to her."

When it comes to relating to Sinners, that's the job description.

Sometimes we stand so close to the screen that the images before us are blurred. We become so focused on the pixels right in front of us that we fail to see the movement of a larger story. Emily, though, standing back a bit, is able to see the movement, the transformation, in Jessica's life. Able to recognize and trust in the Author of Jessica's story, she recognizes that the story is not over yet.

## A Compelling Ride

When I hear rough stories like Jessica's, I often remember another story, one full of grace and hope, that I heard from my friend L'Anni. As she tells it (probably about seventh-hand), there was a guy in Europe—maybe Switzerland, she can't remember—who was a staunch atheist. One day when he was horseback riding, he had a serious accident, falling off the horse and hitting his head on a rock. The man, whom I'll just call Frank, was hospitalized and remained in a coma for a number of weeks.

It's not a very good story yet, is it? Wait for it . . .

When he awoke from his coma, he was as strong a Christian as anyone had ever met. His friends and family, baffled, asked him, "What *happened* to you?"

Frank explained that he remembered falling from the horse. But just before his head hit the rock, everything "froze" mid-fall. Stilled, he saw Jesus, who was the one who'd stopped him in midair, and Jesus began to converse with him. Time stopped. Gravity stopped. All that was happening was this intense, loving connection with Christ, who talked with him about his life. In the presence of such grace and love, the man ended up completely trusting Christ.

I said it was a great story, right?

When the conversation concluded, time and gravity resumed and he was knocked unconscious in the fall. When he woke from the coma, he remembered his encounter with Jesus and vowed to spend the rest of his life going around telling people who Jesus is and how amazing he is. Frank's life changed completely.

Over the last fifteen years, I have returned to this story often in my mind. In fact, it has been a formative story for me. L'Anni, one of the most amazing pastors I've ever met, conforms more closely to the image of Jesus than almost anyone I know. She concurs, "I've thought of this story often when people lament that someone died without knowing and trusting Christ, helping them realize that he is far greater than time, space, and gravity."

I know this to be true of Pastor L'Anni from my own experience. When I have routinely squeezed God into a teeny-tiny little box, forcing him to comply with the physical laws of the universe, she has reminded me that the grace and power of an amazing, majestic, and holy God transcend even my imagination.

This, for me, is really good news.

It's also been very important in my relationships with other Sinners. It has allowed me to acknowledge that I see only one image—which sometimes seems just as hopeless as someone who hasn't yet tasted God's immeasurable love for them hovering on the brink of death—in a larger drama unfolding between an individual and God. In fact, it elicits the story of Jesus himself, proving that even death cannot have the last word over the power of God.

It requires me to trust God.

## A Gracious Announcement

I mentioned that, in the summer of 2011, there was a little buzz online when a petition was circulated asking Howard Schultz, CEO of Starbucks, not to appear at the Willow Creek Leadership Summit. Organizers of the petition had, rightly or wrongly, pegged Willow Creek as being antigay and vowed to boycott Starbucks if Schultz appeared. At Schultz's request, Willow Creek released him from his contract. At the conference itself, Pastor Bill Hybels stood to narrate what had happened for those gathered. Without skirting around the issue, Hybels offered a very gracious explanation of the church's position.

While he did affirm that the church believed full sexual expression is reserved for marriage between a man and a woman, he added something else that ignited my imagination.

"At Willow," Hybels announced, "we honor the journey of everyone who's sincerely attempting to follow Christ."

It was the most beautiful expression of conviction I'd ever encountered.

Even if it's not your conviction, you've got to give him props on embracing a third way.

Since there had been so much clapping in the audience when he'd declared the part about marriage being between one man and one woman, I suspect all some folks heard him say was, "We'll keep you around in the hope we can make you straight."

Other ears though, like mine, heard something different. I heard, "A person's story, particularly their salvation story, simply cannot be judged by human beings. The fullness of a person's relationship to God can't be captured in one grainy photo. God is alive and active and his love is wooing people to himself. We don't decide which stories are good ones and which are bad ones. Instead, God's love and sovereignty release us to honor the journey of anyone who's sincerely attempting to follow Christ."

That's what I heard.

This third way makes room for a lot more people on the path to Jesus. In case that seems confusing, let me clarify: by "journey," Bill Hybels and I do not mean that the road to hell is paved with good intentions. Neither are we saying that lots and lots of different paths—via Buddha and Confucius and Muhammad—lead to God. Rather, to honor the journey of others is to scoot over to the side a little in order to make room for others to move toward the welcome embrace of Jesus.

Unfortunately, formed by a ministry culture of getting people saved so we can move on to the next ones, many Religious are frustrated when folks don't repent after their first Sunday in worship. This is why my friend Emily worries that the faithful Religious, like her mom, will abandon relationship with the ones Jesus loves when visible change is slow-coming, if at all.

And yet, because I just can't find "sad desperation" in the face of Jesus when Sinners don't shape up the way we'd like them to, I'm *compelled* to trust in Jesus by honoring the journeys of others the way he did. Until the fat lady sings.

And maybe even after that.

# 26

• • • • • •

## truth. love. lies.

My husband and I have a friend in campus ministry, Dan, who's worked with students for years and years. When we first met him, we were both a little surprised, and a lot delighted, that he did not behave the way we'd been conditioned to expect someone to behave who had the word "ministry" in his job description. Specifically, students would pour out their lives to him, detailing exactly why getting high and wasted every weekend or sleeping around with lots of people really weren't as bad as Christians had painted them to be. When we learned that they shared the details of this debauchery with him on a regular basis, it became evident that Dan, a follower of Jesus, was operating on a completely separate plane from where most of us "ministering" Religious live.

We'd never, of course, been privy to one of these live conversations he had with students, as we'd never hidden in his closet or planted a supersecret spy camera pen in his office. But the fact that we knew they *did* share this part of their lives with him told us something important about the way he interacted with them. For instance, we knew in an instant that he didn't stand there with his arms rigidly folded against his chest. He didn't step back or harden his face, purposefully or inadvertently, to make *sure* they knew he did not approve of their behavior one bit. He didn't call them ugly names. In fact, his encounters with Sinners sounded a lot more like the way Jesus chatted up a notably sinful Samaritan woman than the way a lot of us have been going at this thing today.

Dan is, of course, the modern incarnation of that hideous creature Jesus had been viciously accused of being. He is a friend of Sinners.

## Crabby Naptime Awakenings

Rather than us taking the time to befriend and know and become intimate with Sinners, a lot of our cursory relationships have been like the ones we have with a stranger who knocks on our front door in the middle of our Sunday afternoon nap.

Though we're not in the habit of pursuing them, these Sinners will occasionally land on our doorsteps. Weary, we grudgingly get up to answer the door. Whether they're peddling some deity or just looking to earn a buck raking the lawn, we're seldom glad to see them. After impatiently listening to their story, we leave them out in the cold and breathe a sigh of relief when our door is finally closed and bolted. Nap resumed.

Most of us Religious insiders have no idea what it is to be standing alone outside the door of Acceptability. If we don't have the benefit of a gritty and scandalous past we may not be able to grasp the numerous times and ways Sinners have had the door to God's home closed in their faces. Groggy, we have no idea how some have suffered, and continue to suffer, the sting of our dismissal.

While we continue to rest easy, we've left Sinners out in the cold. Even if we've tacked on an obligatory "God loves you,"—sleepy at best, defensive at worst—we've communicated to Sinners that God is neither with them nor for them.

Lazy, we fail to realize that the Sinner on our porch was supposed to experience, in us, God's great love for them.

## Reality Check

Were we to rouse ourselves from our slumber, step outside, and really *listen* to Sinners, the way my friend Dan listens without judgment, they'd talk. In fact, I was shocked when I threw out an online request to those who had been identified by the Religious as "Special Sinners," asking them about their experience with those in the church. Plenty of these Special Sinners were willing to email an imperfect stranger to describe their experience with us Religious. It's almost like they'd been waiting for someone to ask.

One shared, "I got kicked out of a Christian college for being pregnant. I was asked not to return due to 'sensitive issues.' They kicked me to the curb."

Another said, "I have suffered at the hands of people who claim to follow Christ. All they have done is hit me over the head with their piety and legalistic judgments."

One reported, "I have had people completely dissociate themselves from me, refusing to talk or even contact me because of my 'chosen sin.' Suddenly people were whispering that I was possessed and condemned to hell."

Another offered, "When I divorced, I got many phone calls from a pastor who used Scripture to condemn me."

A transgender adult reflected, "My depression worsened once I started attending a Christian high school, and I was suicidal for much of my two and a half years there. Every day I was reminded that 'All Queers Go to Hell.' Gays were perverts and abominations; people who wanted to change their sex were sick freaks who were worthy of God's wrath and damnation."

Instead of launching our Truth grenade or choosing resolute silence, both of which slam the door shut to relationship until Sinners clean up their acts, we need to get in there and prop that door *open*. The way we do this is by listening.

No matter how heinous the sin, Jesus releases us to be present to the ones he's just dying to embrace.

## But He *Did* Judge People . . .

Though I find it altogether untenable, some of us Religious—to justify our judgment—still want to insist that Jesus was judging Sinners left and right.

And because it's so very hard to find any evidence in the Gospels, the foundational text for many—the one to which we can point, definitively, certain that we're so right—is Jesus's encounter with a woman caught in adultery.

In our desperate attempts to prove that Jesus really did judge others the way we do, the very best we can muster is an encounter where the very last last last last thing he said to a woman, whose trust I assume he'd earned, was "Go now and leave your life of sin." That's the best we can offer to prove that Jesus was just as concerned about identifying and announcing and judging others' sin as we are.

It's true that we *are* players in the drama that unfolds at the temple. Most of us just aren't playing the role we think we are.

It was dawn when Jesus sat down to teach those who'd gathered around him. As he dropped to the ground, the Religious dragged in a woman who'd been caught in adultery. Parading her in front of the group, they pressed Jesus to judge her by confirming that the law of Moses said that women like her should be stoned. With the weight of the law clearly in their favor, they knew they could kill two birds with one stone: Jesus would be exposed as the Sinner they were sure he was and the woman would—no matter what his answer—become the victim of their angry violence. It would be a banner day for the Religious.

Though Jesus knew the law of Moses as well as anyone, he wouldn't be drawn in to their vindictive trap. Instead, he brought the energy level down by pausing to write on the ground with his finger. Like petulant children, the Religious kept badgering him like we do. "Judge her! Judge her!"

Eventually, Jesus stood up and faced his accusers and hers.

"Let any one of you who is without sin be the first to throw a stone at her."

Though the Religious had begged Jesus to judge the woman as an abominable Sinner worthy of death, he didn't. Rather he let judgment land where it naturally belonged, square on the shoulders of the judges.

Tangled up in the trap they'd set for him, like bumbling idiot criminals, the Religious slunk away, one by one, until only Jesus was left. He faced the woman who'd just escaped death. Her heart was probably racing. Looking her in the eye, he asked, "Woman, where are they? Has no one condemned you?" (John 8:10). I can almost see the light, playful twinkle in his eye.

No doubt trembling, she answered, "No one, sir."

"Me neither," Jesus says. Then he adds, "Go now and leave your life of sin."

That was the very *last* thing he said to her. Before that, he'd treated her with dignity. He'd defended her against Religious attacks. He'd gently corrected her accusers. He'd freed her from imminent death. Simultaneously accused, he'd sided *with* her. Granted the upper hand, he'd stood *for* her.

Given the opportunity to slam shut the possibility of this woman ever knowing or trusting his Father, Jesus instead flung that door wide open.

This is why I think it's a little bit crazy that this passage is used by so many as the *most* convincing proof that Jesus judged Sinners the same way we do.

## Doors Wide Open

Our friend Dan was more of a throw-the-door-wide-open rather than a slam-the-door-shut kind of guy. And in throwing it open for relationship with *him*, he in turn threw open for Sinners the possibility of relationship with Jesus.

Since not all of us are as naturally gifted in the social arts as gracious Dan, I'm delighted to report he uses a *formula* that can be appropriated by the rest of us beginners. You don't even have to pay $19.95 during a late-night infomercial to learn this magical secret, because I'm about to tell you right now.

When the college-aged Sinner in question would wrap up their tale of debauchery, Dan would just ask, "So how's that working out for you?" He didn't say it with a sharp, sarcastic tone the way I might be tempted to do. Rather, with a soft face and warm eyes, he simply queried, "So how's that working out for you?"

The Sinner's sin, for Dan, isn't a deal *breaker*; it's a deal *starter*. It isn't a shut door but an open window. For someone who holds the journey as sacred, like Dan does, it's just another opportunity to be a part of their lives.

In my mind's eye, I see Dan wrapping his arms around Sinners at his front door in a big bear hug, throwing the door wide open, and inviting them into his living room. He offers each one a Coke or a beer or a cup of tea and says, "What do you need? With all the resources at my disposal, I am *for* you." He welcomes them as they are, not as they should be. Then he drops down onto the squishy couch and kicks up his feet on a footstool to say, "I'm here. I'm not going anywhere. I'm *with* you."

I'll admit I found Dan's approach more than a little disarming. The way this whole business about engaging Sinners had always been narrated for me, explicitly and implicitly, was that I had to choose *either* truth *or* love. And yet there was Dan who, like Jesus, didn't seem to be budging on either one. Rather, he held the two in tension in some kind of beautiful Zen-Jesus art form.

If we simply have to trumpet *some* truth during the love, perhaps we could announce the really, really good news that it's in fact *God* who is able to leap over tall sin obstacles in a single bound, and that nothing—most certainly not sin—can keep God from loving every single one of us without reservation. Before we ever get around to objecting to sin, could we not let Sinners know how deeply valuable and precious they are to the Father of Jesus, who is with them and for them?

The reason I believe we can, that we've been authorized to love this radically, is not because of Dan. It's actually the witness of Jesus that convinces me we can.

# 27

● ● ● ● ● ●

## the One who is

When I was invited to speak at my church's women's retreat a few years back, I felt as though I would have some kind of home court advantage. Women would already be pumped up to hear from *God*, and most of them had developed such an intimacy that even I couldn't screw it up. I would stand behind the microphone, say some words, and people would magically hear God's voice speaking to them no matter what I said.

Trust me, time and time again, *despite* me, this is how it goes.

Months before the event, I was invited to visit with the retreat planning committee to nail down a theme for the weekend. After plowing through a few other requisite business matters, we got around to discussing ideas. Several weeks earlier I'd submitted three or four possibilities I thought might work. Though there was really only one topic about which I was wildly passionate, I added the others so there'd be more ink on the page. To make it look like I'd tried. Though I was technically *willing* to be flexible, based on the committee's assessment of these women's needs, I was secretly hoping they'd choose the theme closest to my heart. Toward this end, I'd listed it first, in bold, twenty-point purple font, highlighted in yellow, with several asterisks, to subtly suggest that it might deserve serious consideration.

I was so enthusiastic about a retreat theme titled "I Am for You" because, by God's grace, these four words had effectively transformed my insides and my outsides.

## The Backstory

Being relinquished for adoption as an infant, at birth I lost the parents who were mine by blood. The exit of my adoptive father when I was six, my brother's departure for college across the country when I was twelve, and the leaving of my stepfather when I was fifteen had caused me to believe, in my deep places, that I wasn't worth loving. I wasn't worth showing up for. I wasn't worth sticking around for.

No one who knew me would have guessed any of those things. Though I had hardened my heart for protection from emotional pain, it was not in the recognizable form of rebellion. Rather, the girl-sized armor I employed was my tireless smile, promoting the ruse that I was not sad. I was not mad. I was not afraid. I was not insecure. I certainly wasn't someone who believed she was worthless or who was terrified of being rejected, left, again. Blinded by the glare of my toothy grin, I fooled others and I fooled myself.

In my early twenties, a series of new relationships weakened the armor I'd by then outgrown. By my early thirties, like the licked, crunched, broken shell of a Tootsie Pop, my protective shell had crumbled away entirely. Depressed, undone, I could no longer stifle the hiss of the vicious lies that constantly barraged me, insisting upon my unworthiness. Despite an arduous journey of tears and healing prayer and therapy and medication, supported by amazing friends, I continued to suffer. Ready to throw in the towel, I hit rock bottom when I decided that I had spent just about enough time, energy, and money trying to get *fixed*. I wasn't going to end my life, but I was prepared to relinquish the hope of living any way other than broken.

Before I resigned entirely, I raised my fist to the heavens, demanding explanation of the Almighty. Then God spoke to my heart. Just four words.

"I am *for* you."

In that pivotal season, these four words completely reordered the way in which I understood my past, my present, and my future. They profoundly impacted the way I related to myself, to others, and to God. So, they were sort of a big deal. I began to weave them into my writing. I painted them on expansive worship banners. Hoping the blessed assurance would change others' lives, as it had mine, I even had them printed on five hundred orange rubber bracelets.

## Inconvenient Truth

If the other women on the retreat planning committee—whose wisdom and love for the other women in our congregation I trusted completely—wanted me to talk about something else, though, I would. If they wanted me to share about spiritual gifts or say some words about kingdom building or disclose my secrets for not looking like a supermodel, I had enough confidence in their leadership that I would have acquiesced. Thankfully, though, they didn't ask for any of those things. Instead, they set me free to share this good news about which I care so deeply.

Hand half-raised, Carla, whom I did not yet know well, jumped in. "I had an Old Testament professor at Regent College, and when we were reading the Hebrew text, he had us translate *Yahweh*, the holy name, as 'I am the God who is with you and for you.' So, whenever we'd come to the Hebrew characters for God's name, we'd read, 'I am the God who is with you and for you.'"

The other women mulled it over, then raised eyebrows in acceptance, nodded, and said "hmmmm" very approvingly.

My first sinful thought? *That is totally not going to fit on a bracelet*. The *Reader's Digest* four-word version had been tattooed on my heart. Was there room for more potentially useless verbiage?

In the end, the committee set me free to say whatever God led me to say. Then I skittered out of the room so they could continue with their other business. As I shuffled down the carpeted stairs, Carla's words stuck with me, and as I headed home, I continued to chew on the words I'd scribbled down, allowing them to speak to me.

I am.

I am the God.

I am the God who is.

I am the God who is with you.

I am the God who is with you and for you.

Despite my four-word artistic intentions, this was just . . . right.

The extra words slowly took deep root in my heart.

And though I'm not the world's most genius learner, I gradually started to notice, around me, just how *with*-ness and *for*-ness were inextricable.

## To Be *for* Someone

If I stand on the sidewalk in front of our home, I can see Duke University, home of the Blue Devils. Several miles from my front door, on the far side of campus, is the famous Cameron Indoor Stadium. As most folks in the Atlantic Coast Conference know, Cameron is home to a weird breed of life form called, "The Cameron Crazies." These are the students who are stark raving lunatic fans of the Blue Devils. Before each home game these nut balls don electric blue wigs and dip themselves in royal blue paint. If you're not familiar with the madness, please find them on Google images. Though I suppose they must go to classes sometimes, what I know *for sure* is that these Smurf-like Crazies are FOR the Duke Blue Devils men's basketball team.

They're for them, but they're not necessarily *with* them. Though I'm sure some of the Crazies must socialize with the actual players, on Friday nights or Wednesday afternoons, there are plenty of fans who don't. For instance, when someone has benevolently offered my husband and me tickets to a game, we've enjoyed our back-row seats. We were *for* the Duke players, but by no stretch of the imagination were we *with* them.

You can be *for* someone, but not necessarily *with* them.

The same is true in our more intimate relationships. Last week I was walking with my daughter and describing for her the ways in which my father related to me as I grew up. I remember standing in the kitchen of the suburban Chicago home where I lived with my mom, talking on the phone with him. He lived in Connecticut, and he'd invite me to look up at the same moon upon which he was gazing. In that relationship I experienced the palpable sense that he was for me. Against all odds, he knew the names of all my friends and asked me, when we spoke, about each one. When he visited me he would endure long explanations about whatever my eye fell upon in my bedroom: toys, awards, homework, stray socks, you name it. When I visited him, in the summer, he'd help me choose rainbow colors and combinations of patterns to paint my nails.

He wasn't always with me, but there was no doubt in my mind that he was *for* me.

## To Be *with* Someone

In the opening pages of Judith Viorst's bestselling *Necessary Losses*, she describes the chilling account of a small child.

"A young boy lies in a hospital bed. He is frightened and in pain. Burns cover forty percent of his small body. Someone has doused him with alcohol and then, unimaginably, has set him on fire. He cries for his mother."

Hauntingly, Viorst continues, "His mother has set him on fire."[1]

As thousands of children who endure abuse and neglect know deeply, in the very marrow of their bones, whether or not they will ever be able to articulate it, someone can be *with* you, as near as your mother's arm, but still not be *for* you. Spouses too. Grandparents, uncles, cousins, neighbors.

And it's not just about violence. The spouse who's caught up in addiction or workaholism or mental illness, the one who's overwhelmed by withdrawal or unemployment or medication that's not working right, might all be unable to be *for* another in the way that others might want and need them to be.

And yet in our deep places, this is exactly the thing for which we were made. We long for the steadfast loving presence of one who is *with* us and *for* us.

● ● ● ● ●

During the days I was being prepared by God to share the words at my church's women's retreat, I discovered that though the extra verbiage—God being both for us *and* with us—was clearly not going to fit on a molded rubber bracelet, it wasn't gratuitous at all. It was, in fact, requisite.

In the incarnation God made manifest the transforming reality that he was both with and for Sinners like us *in the person of Jesus.* He wasn't simply *with* us, while being kind of ambivalent in his posture toward us and dealings with us. Nor was God only *for* us, but from a great heavenly distance. Rather, Jesus put flesh, sinews, tendons, and ligaments on the reality that the Almighty is, in every way, with us and for us.

## What Not Everyone Knows

My friend Maria, finishing up her grad degree in counseling, works with Sinners. I suppose we all do, of course, but she's really roped in some doozies. Specifically, she provides counseling services to one guy who's a member of the Crips gang. Another client boasts membership in the rival Bloods gang. She listens to women who battle addiction. It's not a prerequisite that her clients have to be the type of Sinner that make the Religious run for shelter, but it has sort of shaken out that way.

Maria isn't the kind of counselor who just listens, nods, and doodles on a yellow legal pad. (Truth be told, I suspect the unfair caricature exists only on screen.) No, Maria *says* stuff. Specifically, she tells the God-honest truth to many folks who've never heard it before. To those who've endured poverty, to those who've been abused, to those whose experiences have confirmed their sneaking suspicion that they're really not worth much at all, Maria announces, "You are

God's beloved. You are made in the image of God, and God wants good things for you."

Some, upon hearing this, weep. They cry because they had no godly idea.

Amazing truth-telling professionals like Maria, pastors and therapists and social workers, are always second-string players in this story. They're second string because each one of us was meant to receive the message during our formative years from healthy, mature caregivers. Ideally, according to the original design, we would receive this message from the steadfast gaze of an attentive, nurturing mother. We'd hear it in her voice. We'd receive it, like Jesus did, from the lips of a gracious father: "This is my child, the beloved, with whom I am well pleased" (see Matt. 3:17). With their faces and voices and arms and bodies, our primary caregivers would convince us we were precious and beloved. And we'd know through their steadfast witness, in our deep places, that God is good. God is with us. God is for us.

And although that's the plan, none of us will experience it fully on this earth. For some, the gap between our experience and God's good intentions is small. For others, it is a gaping chasm that seems, most days, unfillable.

So, daily, Maria firmly instructs the lost and broken and sinful and wounded to believe that they're made in God's image and also that God wants good things for them. And as God-love oozes out of her pores, she truly is convincing enough that even though the message sounds terribly unlikely to their ears, these Sinners simply can't *not* be affected by it.

Though you can't picture my Maria, maybe you remember the wise, gracious Aibileen Clark from *The Help*. Aibileen, the domestic servant who is essentially raising the two children of her employer, balances little two-year-old Mae Mobley on her lap and looks her in the eye. Mae Mobley's primary caregiver then firmly delivers the truth she has not received from the maternal and paternal faces toward whom her own countenance is naturally tilted.

Bold, with penetrating conviction, smiling graciously, Aibileen gently commands,

"You is kind. You is smart. You is important."

Purposing to imitate the face that loves her, Mae Mobley parrots the words, joining the second round of the chorus, as the two voices announce in unison, "You is *kind*. You is *smart*. You is *important*."[2]

What Aibileen does with her face, voice, body, and heart, and what Maria does in announcing the truth to undervalued others, is what every follower of Jesus is *made* to do. Among those who haven't been valued as precious and beloved, it's our Jesus-propelled mission to make real God's acceptance and valuing and treasuring of them. With our faces and voices and bodies, with our time and energy and resources, we are meant to be with and for others in such a way that we—or the mystery of Christ living in us—convince them of their inherent, utter irrefutable belovedness.

God loves you unconditionally,
as you are and not as you should be,
because nobody is as they should be.

Brennan Manning

# notes

**Introduction**

1. Scott Bessenecker, *The New Friars: The Emergent Movement Serving the World's Poor* (Downers Grove, IL: InterVarsity, 2006), 142.

**Chapter 2 Sloppy Dog Love**

1. For more information on this story, see http://sports.espn.go.com/espnmag/story?section=magazine&id=3789373.

2. Henri Nouwen, *The Inner Voice of Love: A Journey through Anguish to Freedom* (Colorado Springs: Image Books, 1999), 13.

**Chapter 3 Internal Consistency and Secrets for Manipulating People**

1. David Lieberman, *Get Anyone to Do Anything: Never Feel Powerless Again—with Psychological Secrets to Control and Influence Every Situation* (New York: St. Martin's Griffin, 2001), 66.

2. Ibid., 57.

3. Anne Lamott, *Bird by Bird: Some Instructions on Writing and Life* (New York: Anchor Books, 1995), 22.

4. "Was Jesus The Friend Of Sinners" YouTube video, 11:10, posted by BrotherRyanHicks on September 30, 2011, http://www.youtube.com/watch?feature=player_embedded&v=tzJwIAr1xk0.

**Chapter 4 When the Church Plays Weird Theological Twister**

1. If you're a dude, a "lady gift bag" means lots of tissue paper, fancy creams and lotions, notecards, chocolates, and possibly some inexpensive beauty accessory.

## Chapter 6  Little Bit Better Than the Other Guy

1. *Saturday Night Live*, season 32, episode 16. Original airdate March 24, 2007.

## Chapter 7  A Fun Party Trick

1. Will D. Campbell, "Elvis Presley as Redneck," speech given at the First Elvis Presley Symposium, University of Mississippi, August 7 1995, http://www.canopicpublishing.com/juke/contents2/willcampbell.htm.
2. Ibid.

## Chapter 8  Friend-O'-Sinners Jesus Action Figure

1. Since there are so many different versions of which folks are or are not included in this "canon" of sinners, I'll just leave the term *Sinner* unspecified and let you create your own mental picture.

## Chapter 9  Who Even Knew about Exclusive Paganists?

1. Lilia Melani "The Other," February 5, 2009, http://academic.brooklyn .cuny.edu/english/melani/cs6/other.html.
2. Lynette Rice, "Lowe's won't resume ads in 'All-American Muslim,'" December 21, 2011, http://insidetv.ew.com/2011/12/21/lowes-wont-resume -ads-in-all-american-muslim/?cnn=yes.
3. Christina Ng, "Lowe's Backlash: Celebrities Attack Online Over TLC Muslim Show Ad Pullout" December 12, 2011, http://abcnews.go.com/ Business/lowes-backlash-celebrities-consumers-attack-online-tlc-muslim/ story?id=15137910#.UC-wuURFpe4.

## Chapter 11  The Nutty Logic

1. "Macy's Fires Worker for Transgender Discrimination," ABC News video, 1:20, posted December 8, 2011, http://abcnews.go.com/Business/ video/macys-fires-worker-transgender-discrimination-dressing-room-flap -15115740.
2. Andrew Marin, *Love Is an Orientation: Elevating the Conversation with the Gay Community* (Downers Grove, IL: InterVarsity, 2009), 17.
3. Ibid., 18–19.
4. Ibid., 19. The parenthetical snicker is mine.

## Chapter 14  Clarifying My Job Description

1. Marin, *Love Is an Orientation*, 108.
2. Ibid., 105.
3. Ibid., 107.

## Chapter 16  Report as Abuse

1. Kim V. Engelmann, *Running in Circles: How False Spirituality Traps Us in Unhealthy Relationships* (Downers Grove, IL: InterVarsity, 2007), 11.

2. Ibid.

3. Elisabeth Corcoran, "The Unraveling of a Christian Marriage: How I Stayed," November 9, 2011, http://www.crosswalk.com/family/marriage/divorce-and-remarriage/the-unraveling-of-a-christian-marriage-how-i-stayed.html.

4. Ann E. Fedeli, *Are There Skeletons in the Closet?* (Mustang, OK: Tate Publishing, 2012), 41–42.

5. Ibid., 47.

## Chapter 19  Two-Headed Baby Born in Brazil

1. Miroslav Volf, *Exclusion and Embrace: A Theological Exploration of Identity, Otherness, and Reconciliation* (Nashville: Abingdon Press, 1996), 72.

2. Sean Dooley, "Tina Anderson's Alleged Rapist to Go on Trial," May 19, 2011, http://abcnews.go.com/2020/alleged-rapist-tina-anderson-girl-allegedly-forced-confess/story?id=13631339#.UC-92ERFpe4.

3. Elizabeth Vargas, "'All Those Little Faces': Elizabeth Vargas Explores India's 'Gendercide,'" December 10, 2011, http://abcnews.go.com/blogs/headlines/2011/12/all-those-little-faces-elizabeth-vargas-explores-indias-gendercide/.

4. Volf, *Exclusion and Embrace*, 75.

5. Ibid.

6. Ibid., 74.

7. Ibid., 73.

8. Ibid.

## Chapter 20  Moving toward People Who Really Matter

1. Kerry Dixon, "Safety or Vulnerability?" *Red Letter* Christians, January 16, 2011, http://www.redletterchristians.org/safety-or-vulnerability/.

## Chapter 21  Double the Strategy

1. Volf, *Exclusion and Embrace*, 72–73.

2. Ibid., 73.

3. Ibid.

4. Ibid.

5. Ibid.

6. Ibid., 73–74.

### Chapter 22  Fred Phelps Funeral

1. Frye Galliard, "The Scandalous Gospel of Will Campbell," *Race, Rock and Religion: Profiles from a Southern Journalist* (Charlotte, NC: East Woods Press, 1982), 46.

2. Yes, I do realize that this statement is just begging for enemies who despise me to come out of the woodwork. I'm willing to risk it.

### Chapter 24  The Moment Ted Haggard Went Home Justified

1. Dan Harris, "Haggard Admits Buying Meth," *ABC News*, November 3, 2006, http://abcnews.go.com/GMA/story?id=2626067.

2. KUSA, as reported in *Colorado Springs Gazette*, Nov. 3, 2006.

### Chapter 25  Until the Fat Lady Sings

1. *The Princess Bride*, directed by Rob Reiner (1997; MGM, 2000), DVD.

### Chapter 27  The One Who Is

1. Judith Viorst, *Necessary Losses: The Loves, Illusions, Dependencies, and Impossible Expectations That All of Us Have To Give Up in Order to Grow* (New York: Free Press, 1998), 22.

2. *The Help*, directed by Tate Taylor (Dreamworks, 2011), DVD.

**Margot Starbuck** is an award-winning writer and speaker who is convinced that Jesus is wild about Sinners just like her. She lives with her husband and three children in Durham, NC. Learn more and connect with Margot at www. MargotStarbuck.com.

# Keep the Conversation Going!

Connect with Margot at
**MargotStarbuck.com** for more resources.

**Margot would love to be with your group!**

Invite her to your church or next event.